HAVING A WONDERFUL TIME

Having a Wonderful Time

*[My First Half Century as a Newspaperman]

Arthur Hoppe

CHRONICLE BOOKS

SAN FRANCISCO

Printed in the United States of America.

Library of Congress Cataloging-in-Publication Data:
Hoppe, Arthur Watterson.
    Having a wonderful time : my first half century as a
    newspaperman / by Arthur Hoppe.
        p. cm.
      ISBN 0-8118-1145-X
      1. Hoppe, Arthur Watterson.   2. Journalists—
    United States—Biography.   I. Title.
PN4874.H635A3 1995
070'.92—dc20
[B]   95-12598
                                          CIP

Cover design: Bob's Haus
Book design: Jill Jacobson
Composition: Suzanne Scott

Distributed in Canada by Raincoast Books
8680 Cambie Street
Vancouver, BC V6P 6M9

10 9 8 7 6 5 4 3 2 1

Chronicle Books
275 Fifth Street
San Francisco, CA 94103

TO KENNETH E. WILSON,

A GREAT NEWSPAPERMAN

Contents

Note

What follows are *not* my memoirs. As my dear wife says, it would be presumptuous of me to write my memoirs before I'm dead. My problem is that over the years I've written no fewer than six thousand newspaper columns, many of them different. This book is an effort to explain why one man would devote his life to such an odd achievement.

Chapter One

WHEN THE WORLD AND I WERE YOUNG

1960! There's a year to conjure with. I can't believe how much the world has aged in the several short decades since, but now it lies before us scarred by Vietnam, Watergate, sexual revolutions, generation gaps, race riots and assassinations.

But, ah, 1960, when the world and I were young. I had been a reporter for the *Chronicle* for ten years and had just taken over a daily column on politics. Bursting with eagerness, I was dispatched to cover the campaigns of John F. Kennedy and Richard Nixon, jumping from one to the other as the prospects warranted. Here was a battle to write home about: cool, cynical, intelligent, handsome Jack Kennedy versus devious, hunched, dark-browed Dick Nixon. To most of us ace reporters, it was the Shining Young Knight versus the Forces of Darkness. The Kennedy campaign was one big party, while the ambiance that loomed around Nixon was thick with sullen suspicion.

Nixon hated the press, and I couldn't blame him. Each candidate was delivering eight to ten speeches a day, all of them, perforce, basically the same. They would try to work in a new proposal or a new accusation in time to make the evening television news and the morning papers, but they could deliver the rest of their texts in their sleep, and so, of course, could we reporters who traveled in their vans.

Thus we members of the press covering Nixon would sit in the front row, delivering his tried and often true remarks with him. I enjoyed best the part where he would say eight or ten times a day, "My mother used to get up at five o'clock in the morning to bake pies, which she sold for twenty-five cents each—and, incidentally, they were wonderful pies, lemon and apple, all puffed up, but [here he would give a little smile and a toss of his head before continuing] cherry was my favorite." As he looked over the audience, the sight of thirty or forty reporters down front mouthing his words and tossing our heads in unison must have, at the very least, caused his teeth to clench.

Other parts of his standard speech dealt with his patriotic joy on being cheered by a crowd in Communist Poland, his courage in facing a South American mob that spat on him and his noble restraint in responding to scurrilous attacks by Democratic leader Chester Bowles. So as his aides glowered, we on the press bus would sing, to the tune of "The Battle Hymn of the Republic":

> I've seen the tears upon the cheeks of half a million Poles;
> I've been expectorated on in sundry foreign holes;
> I despise the lies about Mom's pies,
> And to hell with Chester Bowles,
> As I go marching on.

I have long held that we have a balanced press in this country: The reporters are Democrats and the publishers are Republicans. Our conduct and the bias reflected in all too many of our stories during that campaign not only reinforced my opinion but certainly helped explain Mr. Nixon's acidity toward the media—an acidity that mellowed only slightly over the years.

Initially, Kennedy's relations with the press were not all that warm. Many of us, I included, were Adlai Stevenson liberals, and we distrusted the smooth Kennedy machine and the tough Irish Mafia that had crushed our candidate at the Democratic convention. Nor did Kennedy's style do much to win our hearts. In mid-September, I was writing:

> The most impressive facet of the campaign thus far has been Nixon's ability to get the crowds to identify with him.
>
> He loads his speeches with such phrases as "my friends" and "Pat and I." And many in the audience

obviously feel that this could be their neighbor or even themselves running for the presidency of the United States.

Kennedy, on the other hand, is a tense, driving speaker, rattling off ideas at a rapid pace. But you often get the feeling there is a brittle wall between him and his audience.

Kennedy talks to his people. Nixon chats with his.

But as the campaign rolled on, day after eighteen-hour day, Kennedy grew easier with both us and the crowds. By late October, when making speeches, he had slowed his delivery from a tense 250 words a minute to a confident 160. He also began mixing a few jokes into his message—self-deprecating jokes that became one of his trademarks as president. At the same time, the response of his audience was changing. Where in the beginning they had listened politely, even intently, but certainly cerebrally, now they responded with startling emotionalism. As the motorcades rolled to rally after rally, we reporters catalogued three distinct types of Kennedy fans: the shriekers, the runners and the jumpers. The shriekers, usually women, would emit a thin, high-pitched note while applauding furiously, presumably unaware of what their voice boxes were doing. The runners would trot alongside Kennedy's open car for block after block, smilingly touching it when they could, as though it were some talisman. Most impressive of all were the jumpers, a phenomenon I've never seen since. They might be anywhere in the crowd. When Kennedy took the rostrum, off they would go as though on pogo sticks, jumping not to improve their view but out of sheer exuberance. "Four-foot-two," said Press Secretary Pierre Salinger, happily waving his cigar, as a thin black man in a Kennedy-for-President cardboard boater soared into the air at the back of a crowd in Burbank. "A new record."

Whether his supporters' enthusiasm created Kennedy's new style or vice versa, I don't know. But I found myself using a new word in my reports—"charisma." Indeed, it was so new to American politics that I felt I had to explain its meaning and Greek roots to the readers. It seemed coined for Kennedy.

As a newcomer to national politics, I was astounded at what the candidates went through in a presidential election. I did my best to describe this rigorous gauntlet we run our future leaders through:

This is campaigning:

The twin-engine plane bumps down, rolls to a stop. And it is the same: the control tower with its tinted-glass windows, the low one-story building, the crowd two and three deep pressing against the chain-link fence, the high school band and the waving placards—"America Needs Nixon"—"America Needs Kennedy."

The door of the plane opens, and it is the same. The crowd cheers, the band plays and the local politicians with the badges on their lapels form a line at the foot of the gangway, grinning importantly and extending their hands.

The hands, there is always a forest of hands.

"We were in Springfield and ..." says the girl with the staff badge on. "No, it wasn't Springfield. That was last week. Where were we last night? Oh, I don't know. I just wish we could stay somewhere, anywhere, for just two days, so the things I wash could dry." And suddenly she looks almost as though she were going to cry.

There has to be a speech, just a short one, at the airport. And it is the same. I want to thank all you people for turning out here to welcome me to the wonderful city of Where Are We.

Where are we now? Hurry, the motorcade is waiting and we're 20 minutes behind schedule. Hurry.

And the motorcade is the same: The convertible or open truck for the photographers who jam together facing backward, the convertible for the candidate, the Secret Service car, the convertible filled with the local candidates, grinning and waving constantly at the crowds who seldom know who they are, the three big buses carrying the staff and the reporters pecking steadily away at the typewriters on their knees, the white-helmeted police, grim and important-looking, sirens shrieking, red lights flashing.

The blacktop road into town is the same, merging slowly into a tree-lined residential avenue, merging slowly again into Main Street. Main Street's the same: The five-and-dime, the drugstore, the hotel, the movie theater, the ladies' shop, the ...

Hurry, we're running 30 minutes late. Hurry it up. Hurry it up.

"Where was it that kid fell out of a tree?" asks a reporter, looking up from his typewriter. "Wasn't that somewhere in New Jersey? Where was it?" He seems angry that he can't remember where it was.

And there on Main Street is the river of faces flowing by in a blur. The candidate's convertible throws up a rolling bow wave of cheers and applause that traces his passage. He sits there on the top of the back seat, grinning and waving, grinning and waving.

Where the river is deepest, the convertible will stop, as though by accident. It is an invitation that breaks the dam of policemen, and the river eddies out from the curb and swirls around the candidate's car, the hands reaching up, grabbing, clutching, wanting so, so much to touch.

"I can't get close enough," gasps the thin middle-aged woman to her friend. "You touch him, and I'll be touching you."

Hurry up, get moving. We're late, we're late.

There's the square, just ahead. The river flows into a sea of faces, covering the lawn and lapping up the steps of the courthouse and the banks and the church.

Get him through and up on the platform. Move back there. Come on, shove. Hurry it up, we're way behind. Hurry it up. Shove, shove.

It's hot (or cold or muggy or rainy) on the platform. The introductions: Our congressional candidate in the First District ... Our able Senator ... and the Selectmen ...

And now, the man who needs no introduction, the next President of the United States. A storm strikes the sea, and the placards shoot up, tossing like whitecaps. Thank you, thank you.

And the speech ... It's the same: "The choice is who can best keep the peace without surrender and extend freedom throughout the world." "The do-nothing party of Harding, of Coolidge, of Hoover, of Landon and of Dewey."

Help get him off the platform. Push back there. Shove. Come on, shove.

"I keep writing September and it's October," says the staff aide at the portable typewriter on the bus. "It *is* October?" and for a moment, he isn't sure.

The motorcade back to the airport is the same. There's a small crowd to see you off. The local politicians are there. Shake hands. Shake hands. Good-by, good-by.

You did a great job for us. Good-by, good-by. An autograph? Sure. To Katie? Fine, fine.

And in the plane on the way to the next airport, the next motorcade, the next speech, America rolls past down below—green pasture, golden corn, gray desert. But you don't have time to look.

There simply isn't time.

While campaigning was grueling on the candidates, it was no piece of cake for us reporters. I was filing a daily column as well as lengthy news stories. At times, my mind definitely clouded over. One midnight, while whistle-stopping through Ohio with Nixon, I finished my typing, had a healthy drink and prepared eagerly for bed. I was occupying what the railroad called a "roomette." This consisted of a single seat, a folding table and a bed that pulled down from the wall. I folded the table, discreetly lowered the window shade, undressed and pulled down the bed. Halfway. As the bed would occupy the entire compartment, there were only two places I could go: under the bed or out in the aisle. Seeing that I sleep in the buff and seeing that the car was crowded with reporters of both sexes, neither alternative was appealing. I must have hurtled through the Ohio night stark naked while holding a bed in mid-air for a good five miles while trying to set my mind working on the problem.

In the end, I simply popped into the aisle, dropped the bed and popped back in, all with my eyes closed. I never knew precisely who observed this interesting exercise, but on my way to breakfast the next morning, a young woman two roomettes down the aisle looked up as I passed and definitely snickered.

Of all the methods of campaigning, I enjoyed whistle-stopping the most, and when it came to whistle-stoppers, the two presidential candidates couldn't hold a candle to Lyndon Johnson. Kennedy had defied the party liberals to put him on the ticket in hopes of holding the South, and the heart of that effort was Johnson's train trip through Dixie. We left Washington's Union Station on a bright October morning. From the rear platform, Johnson delivered his farewell address to a small crowd in his usual solemn tones, as befitted the dignified Senate Majority Leader and candidate for the vice presidency of the United States. But as we descended ever deeper into Dixie, Johnson's slight southern accent grew thicker and thicker.

At the very first stop in the little farming community of Culpeper, Virginia, he was already saying how "mighty fine it is to howdy with you folks and press the flesh." By the time we reached Atlanta, it wasn't that he was uttering words I couldn't understand; he was uttering whole paragraphs I couldn't understand.

But—ah!—Culpeper. It set the tone for our journey. The train rolled into the tiny station with its loudspeakers blaring "The Yellow Rose of Texas," the senator's theme song. A somewhat stolid crowd of about 300 Virginians gathered below the rear platform. Lady Bird Johnson gracefully thanked them for "the beaten biscuits and these beautiful roses," and her husband extolled the youngsters in the crowd to "go straight home and tell your mamas and your poppas and your grandpaws and your grandmaws to vote Democratic. You hear?"

The engine gave forth a whistle and a puff of steam. "Here we go!" cried the senator. And the train backed up. For the first time, the crowd showed considerable animation, jumping this way and that. But the engine jerked again and began to roll forward. It was then that Johnson delivered a farewell line that became a battle cry among the press for the remainder of the trip. "And don't you forget," Johnson shouted as the crowd receded in the distance, "what did Dick Nixon ever do for Culpeper?"

And so it was in Orange, Charlottesville and Lynchburg. We were coming into Lynchburg with the loudspeakers blaring when the senator, not realizing the microphone was open, could be heard through the train and out over the crowd telling his aide, Bobby Baker, "Bobby, turn off that god-damned 'Yellow Rose of Texas.'"

Like the other candidates, Johnson often left the train in search of rallies with bigger crowds. For some reason, his staff scheduled him to appear in a hamlet in the Blue Ridge country of South Carolina called Rocky Bottom. While most of the press passed up the appearance in favor of a larger rally, three other reporters and I cadged a ride from the sheriff of Pickens County, Clyde Bolding, who jovially entertained us during the thirty-mile drive over dirt roads from Pumpkinville with an interesting lecture on how to make moonshine.

"Is it—ah—approved of?" columnist Mary McGrory asked delicately.

"Yes, ma'am," said Sheriff Bolding. "It's illegal. Most folks in the hill country make a steady living off it."

The candidate, whose time was more valuable, descended from the skies in a helicopter. Unfortunately, due to there being no adequate landing space, he came to earth in a field of weeds near Sugar Liquor Lake in the shadow of Sassafras Mountain a good two miles from Rocky Bottom. The greeting committee consisted of a solitary farmer, who hustled up to give the senator the first words of welcome: "What the hell are you doing on my propitty?"

The distinguished senator was standing there, picking cockleburs out of his trouser legs when, happily, Mayor George Coleman of Travelers Rest down the road a piece drove by in his red convertible. "I knew right away it was Senator Johnson," Coleman told a circle of admiring friends later. "I said perhaps he'd like a ride up to the gathering place. He seemed right grateful."

Johnson arrived in time to address the Rocky Bottom Good Will Supper in a revival tent set up for the occasion, although he excused himself before dessert. "You don't know how much I'd enjoy sittin' down here and whittlin' with you awhile," was the way he put it, but he had to be getting on back to the train. We reporters agreed his afternoon's work sewed up the thirty-seven registered voters in

Rocky Bottom, all of whom happened to be Democrats anyway, but what do we northern city slickers know? After all, Kennedy carried most of the South.

Kennedy, meanwhile, was concentrating on the big industrial states where the electoral votes were. And Nixon? For some quixotic reason, Nixon had pledged to campaign in all fifty states. With the election only days away, he still hadn't hit Alaska with its three electoral votes. So on Sunday afternoon, less than forty-eight hours before the polls opened, Nixon, his staff and we bemused reporters took off from Los Angeles for the 2,300-mile flight to Anchorage. Off the plane and into the buses for a rally in an auditorium. Into the buses for a rally at a high school. Into the buses and back to the plane and away we went on a 2,500-mile flight to Madison, Wisconsin. But as Press Secretary Herb Klein told us bleary-eyed reporters, "It's a dramatic way to show he keeps his promises." Personally, I preferred the explanation of one of his top aides, Robert Finch. "What else are you going to do on a Sunday afternoon?" said Finch.

While I was new to national campaigning, so was television. After all the hundreds and hundreds of rallies, thousands and thousands of handshakes and endless cascades of oratory, a good many historians credited the initial television debate between the two candidates as being the decisive factor in Kennedy's victory. Not at the time it wasn't. All the major press was there in Chicago, in a large anteroom adjacent to the studio, where we could watch the proceedings on monitors just as well as we could have in our hotel rooms. When it was over, and a pallid, sweating Nixon had shaken hands with a cool, confident Kennedy, a good thirty seconds of silence descended on the press room while we all looked at each other for guidance. Finally, Joe Alsop, the unbearably cocky epitome of the Eastern Establishment, clapped shut his notebook. "It was a tie," he announced in no uncertain terms, and for a good week after that, the conventional wisdom in the country was that the two contestants had fought to a draw. I was never so impressed by the power of the press—or its fallibility.

Close as the election was, the outcome had always seemed to me inevitable. In those days when the world was new, the young, shining knights always defeated the forces of darkness. I remember how the White House looked on inauguration day. The Good Lord had thoughtfully covered the tired old city with a rare blizzard the night before. The morning dawned achingly brilliant, the sky a piercing blue. Behind its black iron fence, the White House stood waiting like a giant wedding cake, thickly frosted with pristine snow—waiting for its prince to come. What a wedding it was! I slept through it.

Well, part of it. I had been working hard. The inaugural balls had lasted until the wee hours. The inauguration at the Capitol was set for 10 A.M. I was staying at the Roger Williams Hotel some two miles up Pennsylvania Avenue. To be safe, I left a call for 8 A.M., and slept right through it. I awakened at 9:40 and did what any ace reporter would do: I threw on my clothes, raced outside and thoughtfully ran around the block. The snow lay a foot deep in the streets. Nothing on wheels was moving. I repaired to my room, ordered a leisurely breakfast and turned on the television set. I had an excellent view of poet Robert Frost's hair and text blowing in the wind, and I made copious notes when the lectern caught fire. Occasionally, as I sipped my hot coffee, I thought I could make out my friends in the press shivering far below the elevated rostrum.

Because of the time difference, I didn't have to file my eye-witness account of the inauguration until early evening. So after the historic event, I sauntered down Pennsylvania Avenue past the White House to the Capitol to capture a little color. On the way, I ran into some of my colleagues who had dutifully sat through the proceedings.

"Have you heard yet what caused the lectern to catch fire?" I asked those who had been on the scene.

They looked at each other. "Which lectern?" said one. "What fire?"

I sometimes wonder why newspapers spend millions of dollars dispatching reporters thousands of miles to cover world-shaking events when you can buy a decent nineteen-inch TV set for a lousy $299.99.

Chapter Two

NEVER LET THE FACTS GET IN THE WAY

OF A GOOD STORY

Washington and national reporting were new to me in 1960, but not newspapering. On being discharged from the navy in 1946, I took a job as a go-fer for an advertising agency at the princely sum of $35 a week. That spring I married my dear wife, Gloria. In the fall, I enrolled as a freshman at Harvard. After two years and nine months of intensive study, I was awarded a bachelor's degree cum laude and returned home, where I was hired by the *San Francisco Chronicle* as a copy boy—at the princely sum of $35 a week. I love it on the rare occasions when some young person asks me the value of a college education.

Paul Smith had become the boy-wonder editor of the *Chronicle* at the age of 28. During World War II, he was assigned a desk job in Washington as a lieutenant commander in the navy. To see more fighting, he resigned his commission and enlisted as a private in the Marine Corps. He was a short, broad-shouldered, fair-complected and extremely fascinating man. The only acceptable candidates for the position of copyboy were young men who were Ivy League graduates, Marine Corps veterans or scions of the de Young family, owners of the paper. His job interview with me consisted of a twenty-minute lecture on what a tough world it was out there and how newspapering required compromises and even cutting corners to bring the truth to an undeserving public. Why he chose this topic, I never knew, but as he talked, I cocked an eyebrow and lifted the corner of my lips in my best cynical, man-of-the-world smile. Unfortunately, as he rambled on, the rarely used muscles of my cynical, man-of-the-world smile went into little spasms, and I was forced to cover my lower face with my hand. I mentioned this to him years later. "I thought you had bad teeth," he said.

One reason Paul Smith could be so selective in his hiring policies was that the *Chronicle* offered a copyboy training program. For four days each week, we performed the most menial tasks in the office, but for one glorious day, we worked as honest-to-god reporters. After the first edition went to press each afternoon, veteran staffers would go over our efforts with heavy black copy pencils and then confer with us about our sins. In six months to a year, we would be either promoted to reporter or fired. It was a stimulating introduction to the craft.

The superior I most resented bringing coffee to or fetching clippings for was Pierre Salinger. Pierre and I were the same age, 26. We had attended the same Montessori-type elementary school with the unlikely name of the Presidio Open Air School. We had gone on together to Lowell High School, San Francisco's academic institution. And we had joined the navy at about the same time. But we were vastly different. At Presidio Open Air, Pierre was a rotund, finger-sucking, sad-eyed little boy in short brown corduroy pants who wanted to be a composer. I was into athletics. At Lowell, I limited my association with Pierre to a condescending nod on passing in the hallways. For I was striving to become a Big Man on Campus, and he was, let's face it, a nerd. But my hubris met the fate hubris usually does. After three years of World War II, I had risen to the rank of pharmacist's mate second class. Pierre had become not only an officer, but the captain of a submarine patrol boat. While I had gone to Harvard, he had gone to the University of San Francisco, working at the *Chronicle* in his spare time. So by the time I arrived at the paper as a copyboy, he was already an investigative reporter, and a darned good one, even though—hello, little green monster—not much of a writer.

In 1954, Paul Smith left to run *Colliers* magazine. He took Pierre with him. When *Colliers* folded three years later, Pierre was working on a piece exposing the peccadilloes in Jimmy Hoffa's Teamsters' Union. Fortunately, Bobby Kennedy was then running the staff of the Senate Rackets Committee, of which his brother Jack was a member. The committee was hot on Hoffa's heels, and the

Kennedys were only too happy to hire Pierre and his copious files. Thus did Pierre go on to become Jack Kennedy's press secretary, both during his campaign and his presidency.

Yet some of Pierre's vulnerability clung to him all through those years of mounting fame and glory. At the *Chronicle,* he was known as Lucky Pierre or the French Kid. He was generally the butt of his colleagues' jokes—well-meaning, friendly jokes, but he was their butt nevertheless. He would respond by ducking his head and emitting a hissing, defensive chuckle while waving his ever-present cigar, almost as though it were a white flag. And that remained his relationship with the press throughout the Kennedy campaign and during his early years in the White House. I always thought Kennedy himself shared that same fond but somewhat deprecating attitude toward him. I remember an outdoor rally in Kansas during the campaign. Kennedy was on the stage preparing to speak while Pierre and I stood chatting by the press section down below. The first few drops of rain fell. Kennedy held out his palm and looked at Pierre with a glowering, accusatory grin. Pierre waved his cigar, ducked his head and hissed his chuckle.

By then, Pierre and I had become equals and friends again. As a press secretary, he was, to be sure, far more important than a mere reporter in the scheme of things, but no reporter has ever thought so. We had our last close meeting five days after Kennedy was killed. I was sitting in Pierre's White House office. It had been dark outside for hours. The funeral was over. The new president had been sworn in. The last reporters had trickled out the doors. Pierre idly shuffled through the papers on his desk as though looking for one that would pique his interest. He picked up a news magazine, glanced at the photographs of the assassination and tossed it down. "Jesus," he said. After five hectic, sleepless, emotion-soaked days there was nothing for him to do. His assistant, Andy Hatcher, came in, putting on his overcoat. Pierre suddenly reached out and took his hand. Awkwardly, they half embraced. Both would stay on their jobs because the new president had asked them to, but this was the closing scene, the end of a cycle.

I had sat in that same chair in that same office on a crisp January morning almost three years before. It was the New Frontier's first day in the White House. I had ridden in with Pierre from his hotel that morning in his first White House limousine. He was wearing a bright yellow shirt, his face red with cold and joy, an ever-present cigar between his teeth and two boxes more on his lap. How happy he'd been behind his new desk, like a child on Christmas. "Get me Secretary Hodges," he had said sternly into the telephone, and then he had looked up at me, grinning at his own importance.

It seemed so long ago. Now, after the assassination, the walls of his office were covered with photographs and mementos of those three years. He had been sent by Kennedy to talk to Khrushchev. He had gained the respect of the press corps. He was no longer as much the lovable butt of their jokes. Those three years in power had matured him, and now they had sobered him. After Hatcher left, he picked up a phone. "Get me a car, please," he said. "I want to go home."

Of all the reporters present earlier, I was the one he had asked home for dinner. It was not that I was his best friend among them—far from it. It was, I think, that I went back to his beginnings. As the car hummed through the darkness to his Virginia suburb, he began to talk, stiltedly, with long pauses. All he could talk of was Kennedy, of unrelated incidents, with no thread, no continuity. He kept trying to sum up how he felt—not for my sake, but for his own. "I owe everything to him," he said, "everything." He was quiet for a long moment, and then he lifted his head. "He was my president," he said, and we both began to cry.

For thirty years after that night, I never had a conversation with Pierre. He went on to become a United States senator, a distinguished foreign correspondent and a television network executive. I saw him occasionally on television: that great leonine head, that heavy-browed, unsmiling visage, that pontifical bearing. When he came to San Francisco, he never called. When I mentioned this in a column I wrote about him, he immediately telephoned to say he was coming my way and would I have dinner with him. I was delighted to see him. He talked about how he made $500,000 a year with ABC, his new job signing up clients like Arafat for an international public relations firm and, seeing that I was planning a trip to Cuba, how he could easily arrange an interview for me with Fidel Castro. We embraced in farewell, and I never heard from him again. Oddly enough, I didn't mind. He earned his stature, and I was illogically proud to have known him when. His is what might be described as a psychological Horatio Alger story, for he has proved that in this great land of ours, any introverted, confused, finger-sucking little boy can grow up to become an elder statesman.

After seven months of fetching and carrying for Pierre and his peers at the *Chronicle,* I was promoted to reporter with a raise to $50 a week. When I complained mildly about the pay, I was told the story of one Joe McGaffrey at the *San Francisco News* back in the days when reporters made $11 a week. McGaffrey went one day to the city editor to say he was leaving to take a job at the *Examiner* for $22 a week. "You mean you'd quit the *News,*" roared the editor, "for a lousy eleven bucks a week?" It was then that I realized I wasn't in this profession for the money.

The *Chronicle* did what it could to reinforce that realization. In those days, reporters had to ask the permission of a city editor to make a ten-cent toll call to the East Bay. I still claim the most frugal expense account on record—$12.47 for a week-long assignment. This was for a series I wrote on Skid Road. I let my beard grow for a week, donned a floppy-brimmed hat, an old suit coat, aging khakis and canvas shoes with holes in the toes and simply stepped out the back door of the *Chronicle,* for Skid Road began across the street. (Today, it's a full block away, which is a tribute to civic progress.) I rented a hotel room for 75 cents a day, profligately paying even for the one night I spent in a Salvation Army shelter and another I spent in jail.

I found that the life of a Skid Road bum offers attractions I hadn't expected, such as relief from those dreary duties that have been drilled into us since childhood—bathing, combing your hair and brushing your teeth. Afterward, I was surprised that it was this aspect of my experience that men in particular asked about, and the more driving and important they were, the more their interest in this freedom from responsibility.

It was also the first time I had been treated inhumanely. This was the night I set out to be arrested. It wasn't difficult: I poured a half bottle of Tokay over my head and hunkered down on the curb. Along came the Black Maria right on schedule. An officer, wearing black rubber gloves as a precaution against who-knows-what dreaded diseases, herded me in. At the jail, I sat interminably on a wooden bench. Finally an older policeman came along with a key attached to a foot-long wooden stick. "You," he said to me. Before I could rise, he whacked me on the knee with the stick. It wasn't brutality. It was the way a farmer would whack a cow to get it moving. It was, literally, inhumane. To this day, the memory bothers me. What bothers me, I suppose, is that we are capable of treating our fellow human beings, not with hate or fear or anger, but with no emotion whatsoever. It is how the German guards must have felt at Dachau.

When I returned home after my week of high living, my dear wife made me take off all my clothes in the basement and tiptoe starkers up to the shower. I then wrote a series of six long articles about Skid Road. The *Chronicle* printed five. The one they excised was the one I thought most interesting. It was the one on sex. Much of the conversation I had with the poor, alcoholic men I hung out with that week dealt with their fantasies about sex. Not only had they had unbelievable experiences with beautiful women in their past lives, but these smelly, staggering creatures had also had unbelievable experiences with beautiful women only the night before.

What was very real, however, were the well-dressed men in decent cars who cruised the area in the evenings. Twice I was approached and invited to apartments for, in one case, "a wonderful meal and a little fun." In our conversations, my Skid Road friends didn't care to acknowledge the existence of these Lotharios, but, then, neither did my editors at the *Chronicle*.

On my last day as a bum, the *Chronicle* dispatched a photographer to take pictures of me in various sordid poses. The one I treasure shows me sprawled in an alley, raising a bottle of wine in a bleary salute. Over the years, I've sent out at least half a hundred copies of that photo to any commercial establishment that asks for my likeness as an endorsement. My greatest success was having it printed in my 25th class reunion album over the caption "I'm afraid things have a gone a bit downhill since I left Harvard." Not once at that reunion was I asked for a donation.

My other coup from that series was when a city editor, Carl Latham, clapped me on the shoulder. "Great expense account," he said.

So I didn't go into newspapering for the money. I went into it because I wanted to be a writer, partially because, like most writers, I wasn't good for anything else. I stayed in it because I enjoyed being a generalist. Most newspaper people know very little about a wide range of topics, which I find far less boring than knowing a great deal about one. I also treasured the shell of cynicism that goes with the job. At its best, it entailed a healthy disdain for the conventional wisdom, a heartfelt disrespect for authority and a fierce independence. It was something to shoot for.

For the next ten years, I labored as a general assignment reporter, covering the usual ribbon cuttings, commission meetings and an occasional fire. My first big story, the one young journalists dream about, came in the winter of 1953. The assignment was a good one, but not breathtaking: a series of articles on removing the snow from the highways in the Sierra. The photographer was Ken McLaughlin, a tall, slender, curly-haired man with a sweet disposition, a lovely sense of humor and, like most photographers, a penchant for a nip now and then.* Ken and I drove up Highway 40 on a January Sunday. It had been a heavy winter, and already the drifts were a record fifteen feet deep. The highway east of Donner Summit was closed for fear of avalanches, but the plows were still working on the west side. We took our pictures, interviewed the snowplow crews and spent the night in the Highway Maintenance Station at Yuba Gap, fourteen miles west of the summit. By morning, a blizzard was raging. We and our dozen new friends were snowed in. I called the *Chronicle* to report happily that Ken and I wouldn't be at work for a day or two.

"What about the City of San Francisco?" said the city editor, Abe Mellinkoff.

It seemed the City of San Francisco, Southern Pacific's crack passenger train with 221 passengers aboard, had run up on a snow bank and was marooned no more than two miles from where Ken and I sat.

*At five o'clock each evening around the *Chronicle*'s darkroom, the cry would go up: "Mickey time!" Off one of the photographers would go to Hanno's tavern across the street for the "mickey," a pint of bourbon. Cocktails would then be served, usually straight from the bottle.

"I certainly wouldn't want you to take any risks," said Abe.

We certainly wouldn't want to either, so that was fine. The day passed, the night passed and the second day dawned. The blizzard was still blizzarding; the City of San Francisco was still stuck. By now it was the lead item on the national radio news and obviously making banner headlines down in civilization.

"I certainly wouldn't want you to take any risks," said Abe, but he sounded far less concerned than he had the day before.

Ken and I talked it over. We decided to set forth for the train out of sheer cowardice: We were more afraid of Abe than the blizzard. The snow was too powdery for snowshoes. Our highway friends lent us two pair of skis. They posed a problem: I had been on skis once before, Ken never. So we floundered off through the drifts up the highway. Ken was carrying his big Speed Graphic wrapped in a towel. I carried his leather camera bag crammed with four-by-five-inch film plates. After a quarter of a mile, we stopped, cold, wet and miserable.

"I'd give my eyeteeth for a drink," I said in the midst of all that snow-blown wilderness.

Ken grinned. "Reach in the bag," he said. "Reach in the bag."

I should've known. Fortified, we rounded a bend and came upon the railroad tracks. They had been recently plowed! A railroad snowplow must have reached the train. We dropped down into the tracks. With the snow only a few inches deep, our progress was now easy. It occurred to me that the perpendicular walls of ice carved by the plow on either side of the tracks were growing higher. In fact, they were now over our heads. Scaling them would be impossible. If another snowplow came along with its steel blades whirling . . .

Not to worry. After a mile or so we came upon the snowplow. It could no longer do us any harm, for it lay on its side, felled by an avalanche. On past it were the wrecks of two other snowplows. The engineer of one had been killed and his body taken down the mountain earlier. We clambered over these felled dinosaurs and, after another quarter of a mile of slogging, reached the train. It sat there silently, half-buried, leaning into the almost-vertical slope, the snow-heavy mountain towering above it in the fading light. Despite the howling wind, I felt that any sharp sound might start another avalanche.

A passenger was standing in the open doorway of a baggage car, arguing with a conductor. "I don't see why I can't just walk out of here," he said. I remember his shoes. They were black, wing-tip oxfords, well polished.

Inside, the train was cold and dank, the air thick with stale breaths and musty heating fumes. The only light came from red emergency lanterns. The passengers sat glumly in their seats, bundled in everything warm from their suitcases, some with their feet wrapped in torn sheets. I had interviewed a dozen or so when a friendly conductor took me aside to tell me a Sno-cat, which had brought emergency rations, was heading up the highway to a ski lodge. This marvelous little machine, equipped with tractor treads on the rear and skis on the front, was the only vehicle moving in the blizzard. I caught it, and from the lodge called in the story. The rewrite man was a marvelously cynical veteran named Edd (Old E-Double-D) Johnson. His account, under my byline, began: "This dispatch is being written by the light of an emergency lantern in the cold, damp interior of the train . . ." Good old E-Double-D. He was one of the first I heard say, "Never let the facts get in the way of a good story." That was when I realized that newspapers are, in large part, an entertainment medium.

As for entertainment, my specialties as a reporter were humor stories and executions. I liked to say that I was waiting for a funny execution to cap my career. The *Chronicle* has long had one reporter who was assigned to cover dairy queens, yo-yo contestants and the like. Being young, I coveted the slot. As for executions, our reporter in Marin County, in which San Quentin prison lies, was then a woman, Bernice Freeman. In those gallant days, women, by state law, were prohibited from witnessing executions. Because I lived then in Marin, the job fell to me. I was by no means unbiased, having grown up in a liberal household with a liberal's distaste for capital punishment. Here's a column I wrote in 1962 on the subject of killing members of our own species:

> *Scene: The summit of Mt. Sinai. Time: The present. Moses,*
> *holding two stone tablets in his hand, enters nervously.*
> **MOSES:** Sorry to bother you again, Lord, but I'm afraid we
> need another revision in the original copy.

THE LORD: (*with a sigh*) Another? What is it this time, Moses?

MOSES: Well, Sir, it's where You say here, "Thou shalt not kill."

THE LORD: That seems perfectly clear and concise to Me, Moses.

MOSES: But it's causing an awful haggle among Your theologians, Sir. The Catholics feel it applies to spermatozoa and ova; the Conservatives only after the union of the two; the Moderates would reserve it for the second trimester on up; and the Liberals feel it takes effect precisely at the moment of birth.

THE LORD: (*wryly*) Not after?

MOSES: Oh, all theologians oppose killing children after they're born, except, of course, at a distance of more than 200 yards.

THE LORD: Why 200 yards?

MOSES: In wartime, it's a terrible thing to kill a child with a rifle bullet and an atrocity to do so with a bayonet. But all recognized theologians agree that is permissible, if regrettable, to blow them up with high explosives or incinerate them with jellied gasoline, as long as it is dropped from an airplane or fired from an artillery piece—particularly, the Christians feel, if you do so to save them from Godless Communism.

THE LORD: I suppose it does do that.

MOSES: Of course, once a male reaches the age of eighteen, he may be killed in virtually any fashion on the battlefield except with poison gas. The greatest atrocity, all theologians agree, is killing people with poison gas—at least in war.

THE LORD: Then where do they use it?

MOSES: Only in State-operated gas chambers, Sir. It is used there, with the approval of theologians, because it is the most humane way to kill people.

THE LORD: But if it's the most humane way... Never mind. What do you feel I should do?

MOSES: (*briskly*) Well, first off, Sir, I'd suggest You set aside five miles of the Pasadena Freeway.

THE LORD: Whatever for?

MOSES: You certainly aren't going to get the necessary revisions on these two little stone tablets.

Feeling the way I did about killing people, my views were only reinforced by the executions I witnessed. It wasn't that they were inhumane. Quite the contrary. Two guards would lead the condemned man into the chamber, each gently holding a wrist and elbow as though to help him over that last step through the hatch. Behind them came the captain. One guard would strap down the condemned man's legs, the other his arms. The captain would then squeeze or pat his shoulder and say, "Just take a deep breath, Al" (or George or Pete as the case might be). The hatch would clank shut, and usually the victim would glance out the thick window to where we witnesses stood leaning over the waist-high railing to get the best view of his death throes. Often, he would look embarrassed, and rightly so. Except for heroes, dying should be a private experience, as private as defecating. That the state would gather us to witness this last highly personal act struck me as not so much inhumane as obscene.

I wanted to write at length about it. I chose a victim whose execution would be routine. Walter Thomas Boyd, Convict No. A-24708, had gotten drunk and killed his wife. He was a truck driver, but looked more like a bookkeeper—pudgy, rotund, a wispy mustache and (I remember them best) clean fingernails. He was 43 years old. I explained to him that the story would appear only after he was executed, but he never quite believed it. He thought I would somehow save his life. I didn't. He was executed on February 4, 1955, a clear, windless day. I interviewed the executioner, a pleasant, freckled grandfather who had killed thirty or so men, but who averted his eyes from the chamber when he pulled the lever that dropped the cyanide tablets into the sulfuric acid. "I looked the first time," he said. I interviewed the death watch, who took Boyd from death row, stripped him, searched him and gave him new clothing without a belt or shoelaces so that he couldn't kill himself before the state killed him. I interviewed the warden and the clerics who comforted him and the doctor who pronounced him dead. I made notes of every detail down to the small white puff that rose from the smoke-stack over the prison when the poison gas was flushed from the chamber to quickly dissipate in the cold, fresh air.

It was one of the stories I was most proud of—well researched and thoroughly objective. The editors refused to print it. "It'll give our readers the willies," one said. They finally agreed to run it in a Sunday section on the theory, I presume, that readers on Sundays are less prone to coming down with the willies over what is done in their names.

So I launched a personal crusade against the death penalty. Over the years, I've written dozens of columns noting that it doesn't rehabilitate the criminal; it doesn't deter others; and therefore its sole purpose is revenge—a reprehensible emotion in an individual and a barbaric one in a supposedly civilized society. Thanks to my thoughtful, well-reasoned arguments, the polls show more people favor capital punishment today than did forty years ago. Ah, well, I feel the better for it.

*

In 1954, Paul Smith went off to New York to sink *Colliers* magazine and, a few years later, himself. Having gone up like a rocket, he came down like a rocket, spending the last fourteen years of his life in a local convalescent hospital.

He was replaced by the Sunday editor, Scott Newhall. Newhall was an intriguing study. He was a broad-shouldered, squared-faced, wavy-haired man who had lost a leg in the jungles of Central America while sailing around the world on his honeymoon. His contempt for convention was seemingly unbounded. During his tenure as editor, he helped foment a revolution in the Caribbean and a secession in California, launch banner-headline crusades against bad coffee and nude animals, and conduct front-page searches for Pancho Villa's head and a slave to purchase in Africa. Yet at the same time, here was a man who could tell a television interviewer that he lacked the self-confidence to pull the cord for his bus stop, hoping someone else would. If no one did, he said, he would ride on several blocks and limp back to his destination. I believed it.

When Newhall took over, the *Chronicle* liked to think of itself as the *New York Times* of the West. It ran long stories on the grazing conditions in eastern Afghanistan, and its anemic circulation was not much more than 100,000, a third that of our morning competitor, the Hearst-owned *Examiner*, which rightly touted itself as the Monarch of the Dailies. During the circulation war that followed, Newhall turned the *Chronicle* into what was described as a morning satire on journalism. In addition to putting diapers on horses and brassieres on milk cows, he emblazoned our dreary lives with front-page headlines on flight attendants ("CUPCAKES IN THE SKY") and restaurant coffee ("SF FORCED TO DRINK SWILL"). He hired a gay hairdresser, Mark Spinelli, anointed him a count and instructed him to write a sex-imbued column attacking women for the benefit of our women readers. Among Count Marco's more positive offerings were the advantages of urine as a cosmetic and advice on how to take a bath with your lover, shocking subjects in those days. The *Examiner* countered with billboards shouting "DECENCY—*The Examiner*," but as Newhall said, "The trouble with decency is you have to advertise it." In any event, Count Marco was a circulation grabber. As one woman told me: "I can't wait to open the paper to see what that son of a bitch is saying." Indeed, the *Chronicle*'s wild forays became the talk of the cocktail party circuit. Of course, you couldn't talk about it if you subscribed to the *Examiner*, and so it was that we passed them in circulation and forced them into the afternoon field, another victory for irresponsible journalism.

I much enjoyed the small part I played in the newspaper wars, particularly being a foreign correspondent. In 1961, Newhall decided I should cover global affairs and dispatched me to Europe to report on the mood and problems of Liechtenstein, San Marino, Monaco and Andorra. "Take three weeks and spend up to $500," he said munificently. My assignment was to find a patriot in any of these four small republics who was willing to die for his country. I couldn't. "Look," the leading citizen of Liechtenstein said earnestly when I put the question to him over dinner, "I don't even hunt rabbits."

But my dear wife, Gloria, and I started and finished the assignment in Paris, thus affording us a Grand Tour of Europe. I was filing daily stories. When we reached Venice, our hotel lobby was under two inches of water, and I learned the fact, little reported at the time, that Venice was settling slowly into the Adriatic. I mailed in a lighthearted story. Newhall slapped on a banner headline in screaming 72-point type:

VENICE SINKS
HOPPE LEAVES

It presumably sold a few extra papers. It definitely stimulated several panicky phone calls from Italo-American residents of North Beach who had loved ones in Venice.

Not long after that, a brief United Press story crossed my desk saying the new African republic of Zambia had entered the space race against America and the Soviet Union. An enterprising Zambian, the story said, planned to put the first astronaut on the moon using an ancient African catapult system. He was even now rolling his fledgling astronauts downhill in barrels to give them a feeling of free fall. I sent the dispatch into Newhall, and the next morning I was on a plane for Africa. I located the entrepreneur, Edward Nkoloso, an engaging if somewhat insane man, hired a photographer to capture his astronauts in their barrels and mailed in the story. ("HOPPE MEETS SPACE MEN"). I then repaired to the bar of the one decent hotel in Lusaka where a dozen genuine foreign correspondents, most of them British, were gathered. They thought it absolutely hilarious that I had flown 15,000 miles to interview Mr. Nkoloso. They, on the other hand, were trying desperately to get into the Congo next door where a violent revolution was erupting with both sides shooting at everything in sight, including—God forbid—newspapermen. And they thought I was crazy. But duty called, and I went down with them each morning to the Congolese consul, where I would put in my bid: "Please, sir, you don't want to give me a visa to the Congo, do you?" He, thank God, didn't. But it was there in Lusaka that I first heard my favorite foreign correspondent line: "What did you file?" one would ask. "Oh, the usual," was the laconic reply: "'Leopoldville, The Congo—I watched in horror today as ... (pickup wires).'"

On returning from my African foray I was appalled by the number of letters excoriating me for blatant racism in poking fun at uneducated Africans. The thought had never occurred to me. I believed that it was the Africans who were satirizing our multibillion-dollar space race against the Russians. Indeed, I patted myself on the back for being so lacking in racism that I never considered the possibility the stories would be thought racist. I mentioned this to a veteran *Chronicle* editor the other day. He laughed and said that Newhall had told him at the time that the series was "going to be the greatest Rastus story in the history of journalism." I think now that I may have been just plain naive.

But we foreign correspondents do have James Bond adventures—riding midnight trains, sleeping with beautiful women ... I came very close to sleeping with a beautiful woman on a midnight train in Russia in 1965. (And it's about time we got some sex into this book.) A Soviet friend told me that the Russian humor magazine, *Krokodil*, had reprinted one of my columns without permission. I wrote them a friendly letter requesting payment. They wrote back saying that, in the interests of Soviet-American friendship, they would be delighted to give me a check for sixty rubles, but—ha, ha, ha—I would have to come to Moscow to claim it. Well—ha, ha, ha—I showed their letter to Newhall, and I was on plane to Leningrad in no time at all. After a day exploring the Hermitage and whatnot, I boarded the famed Red Arrow at midnight for the six-hour run down to Moscow. Now, there's a train to rival the Orient Express for mystery and intrigue. Clouds of white steam hissed from the huge black engine trimmed in red and gold with polished brass fixtures. The passengers, each obviously a master spy, hustled down the platform in furs and trench coats. I boarded a car and found my compartment. It was furnished with twin beds separated by a night table. A small lamp with a rose-silk shade was perched on the night table, bathing the room in a soft, sensuous glow.

I was looking about for a place to stow my suitcase when my compartment mate entered. She was—cross-my-heart-and-hope-to-die—a beautiful woman. Well, perhaps not beautiful, but definitely highly attractive. She explained in perfect English that she was an Intourist guide who had just dropped off a group of British travelers and was on her way back to Moscow for reassignment. And who was I? An American? She frowned.

"Then you probably are not accustomed to the sleeping arrangements on our Russian trains," she said.

Well, no, I said, but I was certainly willing to learn.

"You see, we think nothing of members of the opposite sex sharing a compartment," she said.

Oh, heck, neither do we Americans, I said. Happens all the time.

"No, no," she said. "I know you'd be embarrassed."

Embarrassed? Oh, no, no, no, not for a minute.

"You're polite to say so," she said, "but you obviously would be more comfortable with someone else."

Oh, no, no, no, no . . .

But she disappeared and returned in a few minutes with a tall, broad-shouldered, blond young man who didn't speak a word of English and who spent the next three hours trying to tell me in sign language and grunts that—as I finally figured out to the relief of both of us—the USSR had defeated the United States 5–3 in ice hockey.

It was on my way out of Russia, after collecting my sixty rubles, that I met the only other attractive woman I had seen in my week in the Soviet Union. And this one was truly beautiful—tall, dark and stately with large brown eyes and, unfortunately, the uniform of a customs guard.

In Moscow, I'd had lunch with Henry Shapiro, who had been the local bureau chief for United Press for a couple of decades and whose clout was so great that he lived in one of the few private homes in Moscow. After vodka, wine and salmon, he asked if I would take an 18th-century Russian icon to his daughter in Berkeley. "Just put it in the bottom of your suitcase," he said. "They'll never look."

No problem, I said. Being an ace, James Bond–type foreign correspondent, I could carry off a minor smuggling like that while falling off a log. I then didn't sleep for my next three nights in Russia.

By the time I reached the airport in Kiev, I was chain-smoking cigarettes and flicking them away while mentally declining a blindfold. But if James Bond could carry it off, by golly, so could I. In the line at customs, the agents were pawing through the suitcase of the man ahead of me. Not to worry; he clearly looked suspicious. Then it was my turn. What luck! I was face to face with as beautiful an agent as 007 could ever have wished for.

"Have you anything to declare?" she asked politely.

I looked into those huge brown eyes, squared my shoulders and said coolly in my best James Bond manner: "I-have-an-icon-in-my-suitcase!"

In a twinkling, I was surrounded by male agents, all even taller.

"Where did you get that icon?" one asked grimly.

Rat on a pal? What kind of a spineless creature did they think I was? "I-got-it-from-Henry-Shapiro-in-Moscow!" I said calmly.

Needless to say, they confiscated the icon, and to this day, I don't give a fig if Shapiro ever got it back. In my defense, I will say that I have warned all my friends that if the Communists ever take over America and arrest me, they would be well advised to flee the country.

By then, I had been a columnist for four years. In January of 1960, Newhall had called me into his office to ask if I wanted to write a column about city hall politics, presumably on the theory that no *Chronicle* employee knew less about city hall politics than I did. At the same time, he offered a sports column to a large, florid, iconoclastic reporter named Charles McCabe, who knew less about sports than I knew about politics. Newhall dubbed him the Fearless Spectator and posed him for publicity photographs perched on a shooting stick, wearing a derby and gazing without much interest at a tangled mound of professional football players. Though we shared a sleazy office with grimy windows in the distant recesses of the *Chronicle*, we saw little of each other. McCabe would arrive each morning at the ungodly hour of eight and pound out the last words of his highly erudite column by nine, just as I was arriving. He would then repair to a local bar where he would drink "green death," as he called his bottled ale, all morning while snipping items from various newspapers. He would have a bottle of wine with lunch, take a nap and go heavily into warm Scotch in the evening, thereby seldom drawing a fully sober breath.

"But I'm not an alcoholic," he told me one day on his way out the door.

"I'm glad to hear that, Charles." I said. "Why not?"

"Because," he said, with a rare, genuine chuckle, "I never let alcohol interfere with my work."

McCabe was raised in New York's Hell's Kitchen, and educated by the Jesuits, but he affected the haberdashery, customs and contemptuous drawl of an English aristocrat. He was anti-black, anti-Semitic, anti-feminist and anti-gay. In social gatherings, I saw him cause others considerable pain. His response to any sort of criticism was, "Fuck the bastards." He had no use for the large volume of mail he received from readers. He would toss it all into a basket, unopened. An editorial assistant named Mike Brown, a gentle, pipe-puffing soul, would compose a soft, wrath-turning answer ("Thank you ever so much for your greatly appreciated criticism ...") and forge McCabe's signature. To this day, when I try to explain to long-ago fans what McCabe was like, many will frowningly offer such responses as "Oh, but I got the nicest letter from him ..." So much for the accuracy of biographers.

Yet he was always kind to me, and, much to our mutual surprise, we were good friends. We had a long talk about this once. We agreed that just as I had to be loved in life, he had to be hated. We wryly concurred that somewhere between us was a normal human being. I envied him his defense. How do you take revenge on a man who outwardly enjoys being hated? Demanding love means opening up to the world, exposing your soft underbelly. How much safer it is to remain inviolate inside your shell. Yet how lonely. Poor Charles.

While McCabe's column was an instant success, mine was an instant disaster. Newhall had wanted to call it "The Innocent By-stander," which I liked, but that heading was already taken by a column in the *Atlantic Monthly*. He settled for "Hoppe in Wonder-land" and the results were as God-awful as the title. The columns about city hall were as puerile as its politics. After several months, Newhall took me to lunch in the sumptuous Garden Court of the Palace Hotel. "How would you like to become our Washington correspondent," he said, presenting it as a plum, "and write a column, well, once in a while?"

I thought that over for several seconds. I loved writing columns, bad as they were. "I don't think so," I said, "but thanks very much anyway." We finished the meal in embarrassed silence, neither of us knowing what to say to the other.

So I went on turning out six sophomoric columns a week. Heaven only knows how long it would have taken Newhall to get up the gumption to put a stop to it all. What saved me were the 1960 presidential campaign and Bill German. German was our astute, cynical, Brooklyn-born news editor. It was his idea to send me hopping from the Kennedy to the Nixon campaigns as the prospects warranted. He was a brilliant editor with an uncanny eye for stories.

I remember best Kennedy's first day as president. I called German from Washington, as had become my custom, to see what he thought I might write about. The day's photo opportunity was the new president fulfilling an oft-repeated campaign promise by signing Executive Order No. 1. It dictated "an immediate expansion" of the staples, such as chickpeas and lard, handed out to the needy under the Surplus Commodities Program.

"Why don't you find out what happened to that order?" suggested German.

I discovered that after our new president had signed it with a flourish as the television cameras rolled, it had languished in an out basket for two days before being handed to an elderly messenger on a bicycle who had pedaled it over to the Department of Commerce, where he delivered it to a receptionist, who duly signed for it and dispatched it to the second-floor office of the Secretary of Commerce, which office, in turn, sent a somewhat fuzzy photocopy down to the office of the deputy director of the Agricultural Marketing Service, who told me, when I finally reached him, that the directors of the various commodity divisions concerned would make studies to determine what surplus commodities were available and which would have to be purchased on the open market, if Congress passed the necessary legislation to do so. I never did find out whether any poor person ever got an additional chickpea or an extra spoonful of lard, but I felt I had gained considerable insight into what every determined president faces in dealing with the federal bureaucracy.

So, thanks to German, I was writing stories about national politics and, perforce, producing daily columns on the same subject. By the end of the campaign, the column was being syndicated in a score of papers and Newhall was on the phone to me in New York asking me not to consider any other offers. I graciously accepted a raise doubling my pay and concluded that mediocre comments on major topics are far more salable than brilliant comments on minor topics. I've been careful ever since not to write another column about city hall.

Chapter Three

Money, the Mother's Milk of Politics

Poor Newhall: He so much wanted a column about city hall politics. It was a subject that intrigued him. Indeed, after retiring from the *Chronicle* in 1971, he ran for mayor, unfortunately without much success. But he was kind enough not to take me to task for my dereliction. As something of a compromise, I began covering California politics, spending a day or so a week in Sacramento. The major news organizations each had a desk along one wall of the state assembly. On my first day, I sat idly listening to a Republican legislator orating on some topic or other when a huge, rumpled Democrat at a desk a few feet from mine rose ponderously to a point of order and—snickety-snack—carved up his opponent before plumping back in his seat. The Republican persisted. Up rose the Democrat. Snickety-snack. Yet still the Republican went on. Once again, snickety-snack. After the third time, this mound of Democratic rectitude turned to me, a compete stranger, and shook his head in mock amazement. "That man," he said of the Republican, "is a political nymphomaniac."

This was my introduction to Jesse (Big Daddy) Unruh. He had risen from the depths of rural Texas poverty. "When I was a boy," he once told me, "my parents were too poor to buy me socks, but my feet were so dirty nobody noticed."

He wangled a scholarship to the University of Southern California, entered politics after his graduation and in 1954 was elected to the state assembly. Once there, he was the purest of freshman legislators, eating lunch at his desk rather than at the popular political hangouts for fear some lobbyist might buy him a sandwich. It wasn't long before he lost his virginity.

"Politics is a tangled thicket," he said reflectively one night over dinner. "Eventually, you come to a fork. The path on the right is for the pure and righteous. It's well marked and easy to follow, but it leads to complete ineffectiveness. On the left is another easy path: You simply sell out to the highest bidder. But somewhere in the thicket in-between, I think you can hack out your own path where you can accomplish what you feel should be accomplished—and not lose your self respect."

I never met a politician who better charted that path than Jesse Unruh. His most oft-quoted remarks were, "Money is the mother's milk of politics," and regarding lobbyists, "If you can't take their money, drink their drinks, screw their women and still vote against them, you don't belong up here." His most often-employed critique was "horseshit," which he flung at Mother's Day resolutions, weasel-worded pronouncements and all the myriad insincerities by which most politicians stay in office.

Few were more efficient at milking lobbyists than Unruh. He liked to say that he would gladly push a bill through the legislature that favored one special interest over another special interest as long as the public interest wasn't compromised, but he was hard-pressed to come up with many cases where the public interest wasn't compromised a little. Not that he used the money for himself. He lived modestly when he came to the legislature, and he lived modestly all the years I knew him. Instead, he used the money to elect young, bright, liberal Democrats. Thus did he deepen the liberal tinge of the legislature, and thus did he foster his own power by ever increasing the number of legislators indebted to him. As his power increased, so did the eagerness of lobbyists to contribute to his cause. Thus does power breed power. By the time he became speaker of the assembly, he was the most powerful man in California, second only to the governor, and some would question that.

He used his power to pass liberal legislation, particularly in the field of civil rights. He used it to reform the way the legislature did business, making it a model for other states to follow. But he also relished power for its own sake. Crossing a hotel lobby would require a good ten minutes, as he moved ponderously from one after another of waiting huddles of politicians, lobbyists and favor seekers. He would listen while slowly surveying the room, then nod or shake his head, occasionally making a quip with his tight, thick-lipped smile, thereby sending the coterie into gales of laughter. I remember once walking down a corridor of the state capitol with him and two young assemblymen. He asked if we would care to join him for dinner. When we agreed, he turned to a short, balding lobbyist who was following in his wake like a dung beetle following an elephant. "Five for dinner at Bedell's, George," he said. "You come, too." This latter invitation seemed only fitting considering George, as always, would gladly pick up the check.

So power breeds power, and that's what makes it so corrupting. Eventually, it corrupted Jesse Unruh. It didn't make him avaricious or dishonest; it made him neat. By 1964, he wanted to be the most powerful man in California without question; he wanted to be governor. He realized that the voters in his safe Democratic district would tolerate a 300-pound, whiskey-drinking, cigar-smoking, foul-mouthed slob and so would his arm-twisted colleagues in the legislature, but the California electorate never would. Thus he lost a hundred pounds, renounced whiskey and cigars and said "horseshit" only in private. He also purchased a new wardrobe that featured silk shirts and shiny green suits that would have done honor to a Southern California used-car salesman. Big Daddy was dead, murdered by that new villain in American politics—the television image. Despite his sacrifices to it, he never did become governor, running unsuccessfully against the unbeatable Ronald Reagan in 1970. Eventually he was elected state treasurer, where he served honorably and well, but it was a vast comedown from the days when he ran the state legislature. He died of cancer in 1987, his obituaries hailing him as virtually an elder statesman. But the passing I mourned was that of Big Daddy twenty-three years earlier. There could be no doubt as to the cause of death: "Horseshit."

In the early '60s, the Democrats in Sacramento were divided between those loyal to Unruh and those loyal to the governor, Edmund G. (Pat) Brown. Brown had grown up in San Francisco, a

Catholic politician of the old school and a dear man. He had been San Francisco's kindly district attorney, the state's popular attorney general and was now its lovable governor. His friends described him as liberal and compassionate; his enemies called him "a towering pillar of Jell-O" who governed with hair-trigger indecision.

I made the mistake of becoming his friend; it cost me dozens of columns, for no one in politics was more prone to gaffes than Governor Brown. In 1962, while flying over the vast Yuba City floods, he turned to the reporters in his plane and shook his head. "This is the worst disaster," he said, "since my election." On another occasion, he and I were chatting at a reception when a woman came up to say, "Oh, Governor, I'm Mrs. Joe McGinty. Joe was with you in the attorney general's office."

"Joe McGinty!" cried the governor, seizing her hand. "Why, Joe is one of my very best friends. How is he?"

Mrs. McGinty withdrew her hand. "He's been dead for three years," she said.

These are precisely the sort of embarrassments I'm prone to myself, and my heart warmed to Governor Brown. It virtually caught fire the day he left office. He had pulled an amazing upset by licking Richard Nixon to become re-elected in 1962, but Ronald Reagan proved too much for his tired administration four years later. It was a pleasant January day when he moved out of the governor's office and out of the governor's mansion to return to San Francisco. That morning, his press secretary, Jack Burby, called to ask if he and his wife could join us for dinner. "Great," I said, "and stop by first for a drink." Burby called again late that afternoon. Could he bring some friends along? The friends turned out to be Governor Brown and his wife, Bernice. Somewhat at a loss, the governor had approached Burby to ask what he was doing that evening.

"For the first time in all his years in politics," Burby told me, "no one had invited him to dinner."

And that brings us to Ronald Reagan.

I first laid eyes on Ronald Reagan in the flesh in the Hall of Crucifixion at 8:30 on a September morning in 1966. He was wearing a maroon sports coat. In case you are unfamiliar with the beloved shrines of Los Angeles, the Hall of Crucifixion is a cathedral-like structure that sits atop the highest knoll of Forest Lawn Memorial Park, that incredible exultation of death that only Southern California could produce. A huge sign outside the hall announced that it was maintained by contributions from the generous public, namely 25 cents per worshipper—children and clergy exempted. Inside the church-like vestibule was another sign saying shorts and similar attire were prohibited, but smocks were available free of charge. Through the vestibule was the Hall of Crucifixion itself, which turned out to be a large auditorium. The wall behind the stage was covered with drapes. A kindly woman employee explained that they screened a vast painting of Jesus on the cross "because of the secular nature of the occasion." And secular it certainly was, for this was the monthly meeting of the Forest Lawn Employees' Association, and a jollier lot of mortuary attendants, burial grounds-keepers, plot salesmen and souvenir vendors you'd never want to hear. Never. Listening to their six hundred voices belting out "Smile, Darn Ya, Smile!" in the Hall of Crucifixion at 8:30 in the morning is an experience I treasure.

It was also a fitting introduction to the man in the maroon sports coat, Ronald Reagan. If he thought the ambiance a bit odd— and I wonder if he did—he certainly didn't show it. He delivered his set speech with the skill and aplomb of the accomplished actor that he was, and in chatting with well-wishers afterwards, he was, as always, modest, boyish and eternally affable. By pre-arrangement, I interviewed him in the soft back seat of his limousine on the way to his next campaign stop. I don't recall what questions I asked or what answers he gave, but as we talked, I had the strangest feeling that there was a glass wall between us. I could see him clearly and hear him perfectly, yet this pane of glass prevented me from touching him in any way.

For the next week, I followed him around the state with a dozen or so other reporters and his small staff. We grew close, as people do on the hectic campaign trail—all of us but Reagan. He was always pleasant, always grinning. But he wasn't one of us. He would try. He would approach us hesitantly to offer us some little locker room joke about sex or marijuana in an effort to be one of the fellows. We would laugh politely, but the jokes weren't really funny, and he spent most of his time off in a corner studying his three-by-five speech cards. No, he wasn't one of us. There was always, for me at least, that pane of glass.

I never quite understood that feeling until John Wayne died, and they began naming airports and boulevards for this Hollywood actor. Here was a man who had never rescued a damsel, punched a bad guy in the nose or fired a shot in anger, yet he was one of the great American heroes of the 20th century. His name, of course, was actually Marion Michael Morrison, but he had played the role of John Wayne on and off the sound stages of Hollywood for close to fifty years, and he had played it well. Similarly, I believe, Ronald Reagan had been playing the role of Ronald Reagan even longer. It's the role of the Nice Guy. There is a good deal of meat in that apocryphal remark the Democrats gleefully attributed to producer Jack Warner when Reagan announced for governor. "No, no, Jimmy Stewart for governor," they had Warner say. "Ronnie Reagan for best friend." All of us play roles from time to time, but I think actors like Ronald Reagan and Marion Morrison do it for so long and so well and with such gratification that they become the roles they project. In time, there is no human being left inside.

There should be no quarrel with a Nice Guy as governor or president, especially the Nice Guy from Middle America, one who admired grit, enterprise and the old-fashioned virtues that made America great. The trouble was that the Nice Guy naturally believed he was leading, as he himself put it, "the struggle between right and wrong, good and evil." On the stage where the Nice Guy strode, we were always right; they were always wrong. The good people must triumph over the bad people at all costs. "Better dead than red" was a dictum the Nice Guy publicly endorsed, in the same way John Wayne might snarl, "You want to live forever, kid?" So I never cared much for the Nice Guy's finger on the nuclear trigger.

But Americans loved the Nice Guy as much as they admired John Wayne. Perhaps we have lost our talent for producing genuine heroes, but we are certainly adept at making them up. Thus did the Democrats underestimate Reagan when he ran for governor. My friends in Washington thought it hilarious that an aging B-movie actor would even be considered. "Only in California," they would say, unaware what fate had in store for them. As for Governor Pat Brown's forces, they secretly did what they could to see that Reagan won the Republican nomination over George Christopher, the solid if somewhat stodgy mayor of San Francisco. Much to their later regret, they got their wish. Reagan's script has since become a familiar one: The Nice Guy, who knows nothing about politics, decides to go to the Capitol to clean out that nest of political hacks who are bamboozling the honest citizens. Reagan played the role superbly. Governor Brown struck back with such attacks as: "Would you hire an amateur neurosurgeon to remove a brain tumor?" Brown, however, was running for a third term. His administration was tired, and the voters were tired of him. The Nice Guy finished first.

Once in office, Reagan presented a lovely target. His press secretary was Lyn Nofziger, a dark, rotund, balding, funny conservative I had come to know and like during the campaign. I included him in a decade and more of columns I wrote on the saga of Sir Ronald of Holyrude and his faithful squire, Sancho Nofziger. The plot, such as it was, centered on Sir Ronald's journey through the Tangled Thicket in search of the Shining White House. A few lines will give you the idea:

> Rounding a bend, Sir Ronald and Sancho came across a huge, bloated creature with a thousand grotesque appendages lying in their path.
>
> "Hola, Sancho," said Sir Ronald. "What manner of strange creature is that?"
>
> "That, Sire," said Sancho, "is a Budget."
>
> Well, Sir Ronald had never seen a Budget before, but he could tell right away that it was something evil. So he drew his famed Swinging Sword, and, shouting his ringing battle cry, "For Decency, for Purity and for Just Plain Goodness," he charged the Budget, whacking here, chopping there and lopping everywhere.
>
> But an odd thing happened: The more Sir Ronald whacked and chopped and lopped, the bigger the Budget grew—until it was the biggest Budget The Tangled Thicket had ever seen.

And so forth. I had written a half dozen of these Sir Ronald columns when, on a trip to Sacramento, I felt I ought to look in on Nofziger in hopes of making amends. I sidled into his office, figuratively waving a white flag, and there on the walls, suitably framed, were the Sir Ronald columns. Nofziger beamed at me. "I really know how to hurt a guy, don't I?" he said.

As the years passed, I had to abandon the Sir Ronald columns, for Reagan all too clearly came to know what he was doing. True, like most politicians, he managed to run for re-election—both as governor and president—against the government he had been governing. Even to the end of his presidency, after twenty-two years in politics, he cloaked himself in the remnants of an aura of the honest citizen up against the professional wheelers and dealers. I never cared much for his policies. His mindless anti-Communism frightened me, and his coddling of the rich appalled me. "The country's going to hell in a handbasket," I kept saying, as prosperity stubbornly soared. But I feel much better, thank you, now that the nation is trillions of dollars in debt. As to the image Reagan projected, I was ambivalent. Reagan was a challenge to a dictum I've always admired ever since John Fischer, then the editor of *Harper's*, first set it down: "I never met a politician I didn't like," he wrote, "or an actor that I did."

Chapter Four

Strange Native Customs in Washington

& Other Savage Lands

Washington in the early '60s was both the mighty capital of the free world and a sleepy Southern town. With the exception of the Georgetown cement plant, the only industry was government. Those who labored in its higher levels spent their working hours in partisan battles and devious machinations to create earth-shaking policies that would alter the lives of millions. But as far as culture was concerned, they might as well have been sitting on front porches in Dubuque. Before the Kennedys remolded Washington in their image, restaurants were busy only at lunch, and, when you mentioned the theater, it was to ask what movie was playing at the Bijou. As to its being southern, the residents were so convinced that they lived in the land of magnolia blossoms that they refused to believe it ever snowed, which it did at least several times a year. At the descent of the first flake, Washingtonians would abandon their offices and their schools to flee for home as though a Godzilla of a glacier were roaring down on the defenseless community. As to snow removal, their attitude was: The Good Lord brought it, let the Good Lord take it away.

Politics, of course, was virtually the sole topic under discussion, and being well informed was essential. You felt required to read the *Washington Post* and glance at the *New York Times* every morning, and if you were invited to someone's home for dinner, you never set forth until viewing the seven o'clock news on television.

At the same time, the permanent residents were peculiarly apolitical. At each change of administrations, the tavern owners would take down the portrait of the past president from over their bars and hang the portrait of the incoming one—the way a small town in the Balkans would respond to the arrival of a new occupying force. I was surprised to find that even in such highly political institutions as the White House, the same little cadre of permanent employees had been churning out press releases extolling the virtues of the president, Republican and Democrat alike, for decades.

Congress ran local affairs with a fine, bipartisan and very heavy hand. Consequently, whiskey, tobacco and taxis were cheap. Public transit, which congressmen didn't take, was haphazard, but when our legislators carved Dulles Airport out of the rolling hills of Virginia, they constructed a four-lane super-freeway that went to its doors and nowhere else, thereby preventing Virginians from cluttering up the roadway with their cars.

Even then, it was as though there were two units of currency in Washington: the Dollar, which was used to purchase whiskey, tobacco and taxis, and the Million Dollar, which was tossed about in vast numbers on Capitol Hill. The Billion Dollar was just coming into vogue, and there was even talk of a Trillion Dollar, but only in reference to the national debt. The essential characteristic of this currency was its unreality. No congressman, to my knowledge, had ever seen a million dollars, and thus it was regarded as having little value. That this attitude prevails is attested to by Congressman David Obey, a Wisconsin Democrat. A few years ago, Congressman Obey was questioned as to why he was pushing through an appropriation to build parochial schools in France for displaced students from North Africa. The congressman was indignant. "It's only a lousy $8 million," he snapped testily, and he declined to discuss the matter further. To see how divorced from reality Washington remains, we should note that it would take the average taxpayer 2,000 years to pay for these French parochial schools in real money.

I was fascinated not only by the political battles being waged on the Hill, but by the Machiavellian maneuvers that the occupants of even lowly government offices employed to secure their advancement. I wasn't interested so much in who shafted whom, but how. I thought the backstabbings barbaric, and I wrote a whole series of columns entitled "Strange Native Customs in Washington & Other Savage Lands." Mostly, I fear, I was displaying my own naiveté, and

Washington was no more sanguinary than General Motors. My Sainted Mother used to say that men (and today, of course, women) were driven by one of three goals—money, power or megalomania. I came from the land of megalomania. We reporters were characterized by a burning desire to avoid climbing the corporate ladder. The only way to the top on the writing side of a newspaper is to become an editor. On the rare occasions I was assigned to fill in on the city desk for some ailing assistant, I felt demeaned. To be selected as an editor meant you were the least accomplished writer available. And we, by golly, were writers. Consequently, backstabbing in the reporting business was at a minimum. Thus, when I was told of such stratagems in Washington as "copy to-ing," I found them fascinating. (For the benefit of those who work in service stations or puddle steel, I should explain what copy to-ing involves: A sends a memo to his boss praising the work of B. At the bottom he types "Copy to B," and the copy does, indeed, go to B. But at the bottom of the original to the boss, A scrawls "In all honesty, I should add that B is a muffin-brained chowderhead who thoroughly squirreled the deal.") I would conclude each of these columns with some supposedly satiric platitude on how we should strive to eradicate these savage customs by bestowing on the primitive Washington natives the moral tenets of a civilized society. I only hope that the readers who worked in the towering offices at the pinnacles of the free enterprise system found my innocence refreshing.

I was visiting Washington a couple of times a month. I had found a hotel with an impressive name, the Claridge. The location was ideal—next door to the Peace Corps on Connecticut Avenue, just across Lafayette Park from the White House. The amenities, unfortunately, were minimal. It was a run-down, ten-story building with a creaky elevator run by a sweet, sad-faced black man named James and a cranky phone system presided over by crotchety desk clerk named Hank. A suite—living room, bedroom and rust-stained kitchen—was $12 a day. I fell into a routine that I came to believe was similar to many a Washington worker: I would spend my mornings calling people to arrange lunch and my afternoons calling people to arrange dinner. It was difficult to find time to write a daily column.

My friends in Washington were the reporters I had met during the campaign, a few colleagues from the *Chronicle* who had wound up in the hierarchy of the Peace Corps and a dozen Democratic staff people from California who had come East with Kennedy's victory. Most of this last group had worked for Governor Pat Brown. Their nominal leader was Fred Dutton, a thin-haired, plain-faced, bespectacled man with one of the finest minds I've ever encountered. A Los Angeles lawyer, he had been Governor Brown's top aide and was generally hailed as the brains of that administration. He had jumped on the Kennedy bandwagon early and played a major role in the campaign. His reward was a job in the White House as secretary of the cabinet. I never thought his precise, analytical personality melded with the rough-tough Irish Mafia who surrounded Kennedy. In any event, he soon transferred over to Foggy Bottom, where he served as assistant secretary of state for congressional relations for the remainder of the Kennedy years.

Dutton was one of the two men in politics I completely trusted. The other was Cap Weinberger, who much later became secretary of defense. In those early years, if I wanted to know what was really going on in Republican circles, I would ask Weinberger; in Democratic circles, I would ask Dutton. Why was Kennedy making a campaign swing through the South? Dutton would tell me all he could without violating confidences, and he would painstakingly lay out the pros and cons of each reason advanced. Weinberger was the same. Both struck me as inherently honest men. Even so, I wasn't shocked when Weinberger was indicted for lying to Congress over the Iran-Contra affair. I attributed his misdeeds, if any, to his loyalty to President Reagan, an attribute of honest men. I must admit, however, that I was just a wee bit surprised when Dutton, a lifelong crusader for liberal causes, suddenly signed on as a $200,000-a-year lobbyist for Saudi Arabia.

"Fred!" I cried in horror. "What have you done?"

He chuckled a slightly embarrassed chuckle. "My camel came in," he said.

While Dutton was the leader of this transplanted California group, the center of its attention was Dick Tuck. Now there's a name that will bring a nostalgic smile to the lips of many an old-time Democrat. All through the '60s and early '70s, newspaper stories referred to "Dick Tuck, the Democratic prankster." It virtually became his official title.

I first met Tuck at a Nixon rally in a Greensboro, North Carolina, baseball stadium. A stocky man of about 35 with curling brown hair, cherubic cheeks and innocent eyes approached the press stand. He was wearing a dark blue suit and a badge that said Fire Marshal.

"I understand you fellows want an official crowd estimate," he said with a most serious frown. "Well, I'd put it right on 25,000."

Now this was major news, for Kennedy had drawn 30,000 in Greensboro earlier in the campaign, and we ace reporters viewed crowd estimates with all the reverence the oracle at Delphi bestowed on sheep entrails. At this point, Nixon's press secretary, Herb Klein, appeared to angrily inform us that this was no fire marshal, this was Dick Tuck. While Tuck melted into the crowd, Klein went off to find us an *official* official crowd estimate. He returned with the local sheriff who put the number not at 25,000 but at 20,000. Tuck was only too happy to tell us later, "What did Herb expect from a sheriff who was a county Democratic committeeman?"

Now that's a Tuck story, one of dozens that have been recounted in the national press and told and retold wherever old Democrats gather. In each, a puckish Dick Tuck cleverly bests the methodical plans of the stuffy Republicans. Some Tuck stories are true, some are partially true and some Tuck has woven out of whole cloth. Yet their veracity really doesn't matter. Throughout those decades of campaigning, they served to boost the morale of the candidates' staffs and kindle warm relations with the traveling press. When Tuck was aboard a bus, a train or a plane, the ambiance glowed. Early on, I learned never to question a Tuck story. Question a Tuck story? That would be like refusing to clap for Tinkerbell.

But now, perhaps, it would be permissible to—if you will forgive a change in metaphor—tug a bit at the curtains that veil Tuck's wizardry. I've heard that fire marshal story countless times over the years, and I've told it as often myself. Yet all I really remember of it is Tuck announcing his official count. I doubt if Herb Klein intervened because most of the national press already knew and enjoyed Tuck, and I suspect the Democratic sheriff was a product of Tuck's search for a climax. Yet why shouldn't it be true?

In the years that followed, Tuck and I became good friends. We traveled together, campaigned together and partied together from L.A. to New York. I was as close to him, I think, as any other man was, yet I can't tell you how he lived. Occasionally, a candidate would hire him for a campaign, but those jobs were, perforce, far between. Otherwise…"I am independently poor," Tuck would say when pressed. As I was usually on an expense account, he would allow me to pick up the cab fares, the room bills and an occasional dinner check, but he never asked to borrow money, and he always seemed to have enough cash to get by. When not campaigning, he lived in what became known as "Tuck rooms." These were rooms in houses or apartments across the country that were always available to Tuck. Most of them belonged to attractive single women, for Tuck was catnip to the other sex. Most, of course, wanted to reform him, and many were so determined to do so that they even contemplated marriage. "I can't wait until my Kansas interlocutory becomes final," was one of Tuck's standard lines. "It's only another sixteen years."

One of the Tuck rooms was in our house in San Francisco. My family and I lived in an old three-story home on a quiet residential street. It boasted a small room some fifteen feet above the trades-men's alley. In it, we kept a sofa, a television set and the children's toys. How delighted we were to come down in the morning on occasion to find Tuck on the sofa and the brown leather carry-on bag that contained all his worldly possessions on the floor. We always made sure that window was unlocked and the drainpipe next to it securely attached to the exterior wall. Tuck was a marvelous house guest. He would perform little chores unasked, but he basically paid his keep by brightening our lives with witticisms, inside political information and usually accurate prognoses. If women were attracted to him because they wanted to reform him, men admired his irre-sponsibility. Burdened as we were with time cards and orthodontists' bills, his vagabond ways represented an escape we could only envy. While he'd always talk about his grandiose plans—a movie, a book, a campaign for this office or that—he rarely spoke about his past.

Once, when we were on an airplane flying somewhere or other, I suggested doing a magazine piece on him. Tuck, never averse to publicity, said that was a great idea.

"But I'll need the biographical details," I said.

"Sure," he said. "We'll run through them once straight, and then we'll go back and jazz them up."

I took out my pencil and notebook. "OK," I said, "where were you born?"

"Where's a good place?" said Tuck.

I folded my notebook and put it back in my pocket.

Several years later, however, I relented and did write a piece on Tuck. I sent the original to *Harper's* and a copy to Tuck in case he had any corrections. A month or so went by, and in the same day's mail, I received two items of interest: a polite letter of rejection from *Harper's* and a copy of *Washingtonian* magazine featuring my piece on Tuck. They had printed it word for word except for a paragraph I'd never seen before extolling Tuck's fantastic appeal on the lecture circuit and announcing that he was available for a thousand dollars a shot. "Those imaginative editors," he said. "Always beefing up the copy." Well, I suppose I should be glad *Harper's* rejected the piece so that it didn't appear twice on the same newsstands. I know I was pleasantly surprised when I, and not Tuck, received the check from the *Washingtonian.*

Meanwhile, the Tuck stories accumulated. I have the physical proof of one of the early ones—the pieces of a three-by-four-foot placard that reads in large letters: "WELCOME NIXON." Below that is a line in Chinese characters. This was during Nixon's 1962 campaign for governor of California. There was talk that Nixon had surreptitiously accepted a large loan from Howard Hughes' Hughes Tool Company for his brother. The media had been playing it down, and the Democrats were doing their utmost to bring it out in the open. Nixon was making an appearance in Los Angeles' Chinatown when three small boys, one of them carrying the sign, approached him. As all good politicians should, Nixon put his arms around these young supporters and beamingly posed for the television cameras. "No, no!" cried a horrified Chinese elder, rushing forward to snatch the sign and tear it to bits. For the line in Chinese said, "What about the huge loan?"

"How about that?" said Tuck afterwards. "There's no way to say 'Hughes' in Chinese."

It was during that same campaign that a classic Tuck story, "Dick Tuck and the Runaway Train," evolved. Nixon was whistle-stopping through California, and Tuck was racing the train in a convertible driven by an attractive young woman. He managed to appear at most stops before the train arrived. At one stop, he and I were reminiscing about the incident in 1960 when Lyndon Johnson's train backed up into the crowd in Culpeper, Virginia. "It would be funnier," Tuck mused, "if the train had pulled out while Johnson was still speaking."

Sure enough, when the Nixon train arrived at the next stop in San Luis Obispo, there was Tuck, wearing his dark blue suit, plus a newly acquired engineer's cap, and carrying a red lantern. He was standing some twenty yards up the track from the rear platform, where Nixon was addressing the crowd. After a dozen or so of us reporters gathered around him, Tuck waved his lantern and shouted, "Okay, move her out!" Needless to say, nothing happened, but as the story has been told and retold for all these years, the train dutifully chugged out of the station with Nixon ranting with clenched fists at its crew.

Another campaign, another train, another Tuck story: In 1964, Tuck hired a lovely young woman, Moira O'Conner, to pose as a news-paper reporter and distribute anti-Goldwater propaganda under the compartment doors aboard the candidate's whistle-stop special as it thundered through Ohio in the dead of night. Unfortunately—or perhaps fortunately for Tuck—she was caught red-handed by a Goldwater aide, who was quoted in the press as saying in the most fitting conservative-Republican manner "I think you have made your last delivery, my dear." She quickly broke and named Tuck as the mastermind who ran her. Tuck's name and photograph were prominently displayed in newspapers across the country. This shows either (a) how adroit Tuck was in manipulating the press or (b) what a dull campaign it was.

National reporters were inordinately fond of Tuck. He not only brightened their duties with his ploys and witticisms, he was genuinely helpful. A small example: At the Al Smith Dinner at the

Waldorf Hotel in 1960, at which both Nixon and Kennedy were speaking, a self-important official at the door adamantly refused to let a dozen or so of us reporters into the black-tie affair. We had argued and pleaded for a good five minutes when suddenly Tuck appeared behind this guardian of the gate and tapped him on the shoulder. "That the press?" asked Tuck in his most stern and officious manner. "Okay, let 'em in." And let us in the man did.

At the Republican Convention in 1964, the television anchormen high in their booths commented frequently on how crowded the convention floor had become. One reason was that Tuck was handing out treasured floor passes to all his friends in the media. "Careful," he said, as he offered me mine. "The ink's still wet."

When Tuck launched a quixotic campaign for the California state senate in 1966, I wasn't surprised when his friends in the national press corps threw a gala fundraising ball for him in Washington. The slogan was: "The Job Needs Tuck, and Tuck Needs the Job." Virtually every big name in journalism turned out, and a check for $3,000 helped supply Tuck's storefront headquarters in Los Angeles with mimeograph paper, vodka and other office supplies.

It was a joyful campaign. Even Nixon played a part. One thing I've discovered after all these years of using humor to attack politicians is that they are compelled not to take umbrage. No matter how seething they may be inside, they must grit their teeth and smile bravely for fear they would be accused—God forbid!—of having no sense of humor. Nixon always contended that he liked Tuck—preferably, I thought, parboiled. Though he had been the target of dozens of Tuck's pranks, on the surface Nixon actually seemed to enjoy him. Spotting Tuck among the reporters at a press conference in Los Angeles in 1962, Nixon pointed to him, grinned and said, "The last time I saw Dick Tuck, he was in a Nixonette costume." Tuck, never at a loss, whispered to his friends "Yeah, but ask him how he found out it was me under that skirt."

Given that relationship, I suggested to Tuck that we seek Nixon's endorsement in Tuck's senate race. "That ought to kill any chance you have in this heavily Democratic district," I said. "He'll leap at it."

"Great idea," said Tuck.

So we drove down to Newport Beach, where Nixon, then at the nadir of his career, was speaking to a small meeting of Republican faithful. Tuck waited in the car while I cornered Nixon after his speech to explain my mission. Nixon grasped the situation instantly.

"I've thought about it," he said with a smile of pure delight. But then he frowned. "But I'm afraid I must follow my usual rule of not intervening in the primaries."

A crying shame, I said, for I saw the possibilities of a column on the subject flying out the window. But I had underestimated Nixon. He, in effect, wrote the column for me.

"True," Nixon went on without a moment's hesitation, "Tuck threw some very nice needles at me during the '60 and '62 campaigns, but I learned to enjoy him personally, and I don't feel any animosity toward him. Besides, that blithe spirit should not be snuffed out. Thinking of the public interest, I will say that every legislature needs a Dick Tuck. His election would certainly make Sacramento one of our most interesting state capitals. Naturally, I'm for the Republican, but if it has to be a Democrat, why not Tuck?"

Was he then giving Tuck his blessing? I asked hopefully.

"In a left-handed way," he said, his smile now a grin. "In fact, I may sum up my position best by saying I come not to bury Dick Tuck, but to praise him."

I felt that should certainly do it, and I handed the former vice president a photograph of himself that Tuck had asked me to have autographed. Nixon whipped out a pen and, without even blinking, scribbled "To Dick Tuck—May he get in the coming election everything he deserves."

Say what you will about Nixon—and everyone has—I take issue with those who claim he has no sense of humor.

Needless to say, Tuck did get what he deserved in that election, although he claims he's still waiting for the farm vote to come in. In the end, however, Nixon unintentionally wreaked his revenge. His revenge was Watergate. After the nation had been put through that seamy mess, political trickery of any sort—even Tuck's merry pranks—was eschewed by both parties at all costs, and Tuck, at the last sighting, was living the life of a gentleman farmer in Parachute, Colorado.

But Watergate brings us to our last Tuck story. Bob Haldeman, Nixon's tough chief of staff, was just emerging from a sweaty session in a Senate hearing room when he ran into Tuck in the corridor.

"You started all this, Tuck," Haldeman supposedly said.

"Maybe so," said Tuck, "but you ran it into the ground."

And so they did.

Chapter Five

JUST PLAIN JACK

President Kennedy proved a tempting subject for a satirical columnist new to the Washington scene. I started a series of columns that began "Good morning, housewives and other shut-ins. It's time for another episode of 'Just Plain Jack,' the heartwarming story of one young man's struggles to overcome the handicaps of good looks and incredible wealth."

The main characters in this running soap opera were the Beautiful Society Girl He Married, Portly Pierre, the faithful family retainer and, of course, Just Plain Jack. In those days, "jack" was a synonym for money, and I must admit I was somewhat nonplused when, after turning out a score of these brilliantly witty pieces, an elderly woman told me, "I just love your series on Just Plain John." Each chapter would end with a little homily based on this double-entendre, such as "And meanwhile, as you meander down the pathways of life, folks, remember: When it comes to winning public approval, you can always depend on Just Plain Jack."

What may seem odd today is that these innocuous columns stirred a storm of angry letters. "How can you deride our president like that?" was the general theme. The nation was then just emerging from the roseate glow of the Eisenhower years, where Norman Rockwell set the taste in satire. Black humor in greeting cards had yet to make its appearance, and when Mort Sahl made jokes about our president practicing golf swings in the Oval Office, several members of the audience actually gasped.

But times were beginning to change, and I had no compunctions about gently attacking Kennedy, for I was no great fan of his as a politician. After all, I was one of those death-wish liberals who had rooted for Adlai Stevenson through two losing presidential campaigns against Ike and a losing race against Kennedy for the nomination at the Democratic Convention in Los Angeles in 1960. Down deep, we death-wish liberals were buoyed up every time our candidate lost, for if he had won, it would indicate the majority was just as smart as we were. Perhaps it went hat in hand that we were also politically ineffectual. One of our intellectual leaders was Harry Girvetz, a philosophy professor at the University of California at Santa Barbara. It was Girvetz who had 10,000 fortune cookies printed with the message "Your Future Lies with Adlai." He distributed a thousand as the 1960 convention opened and, exhibiting the political acumen of a good liberal, saved the other 9,000 for the crucial second ballot. It is said that Professor Girvetz passed away late in life with a garage full of fortune cookies.

As I've grown older, I've perhaps become more of an anarchist than a liberal, but you have to have a warm spot for an entire class of people who have hearts that bleed. Here's a column from 1968:

> *Scene: The Pearly Gates. St. Peter, the Heavenly Roll in hand, awaits as a weary figure trudges up the marble steps.*
> St. Peter: Your name, please?
> Mr. Liberal: Liberal. Alfred J. Liberal. (*nervously*) But I'm not sure I belong here.
> St. Peter: We'll be the judge of that, Mr. Liberal. Now if you will recount your good deeds.
> Mr. Liberal: Good deeds? Let's see, good deeds. Well, when I was young, I attended benefit banquets. You know, for starving Armenians and things. And a lot of charity balls, like for crippled children ...
> St. Peter: (*making notes*) Ate for the hungry, danced for the crippled. What about the poor and oppressed?
> Mr. Liberal: Oh, I hardly remember a cocktail party where I didn't argue strongly for welfare legislation. And I always defended the underdog, too—the Loyalists in Spain, the Jews

in Germany, the Vietnamese in Vietnam and, of course, the Neg ... Excuse me, the blacks.

ST. PETER: The blacks?

MR. LIBERAL: (*enthusiastically*) Oh, yes, the one big thing in my whole life was helping the Neg ... Excuse me, the blacks. Why, back in the '40s I was the first in my neighborhood to have one to dinner. Ah, those were the days.

ST. PETER: (*making a note*) Drank for the poor, fed a black.

MR. LIBERAL: (*proudly*) I was a life-long member of the National Association for the Advancement of Colored People. Then, when the Colored People advanced, I joined the Urban League and CORE and Friends of SNCC. But pretty soon, they didn't ask me to speak anymore. Instead, young men in overalls would stand up and call us yellow-livered Honkies.

ST. PETER: And how did you retaliate?

MR. LIBERAL: Oh, I applauded, of course. (*frowning*) Then they threw me out. Quite rightly, too.

ST. PETER: What did you join then?

MR. LIBERAL: (*shrugging*) There wasn't much left. ADA split up. The labor unions were fat. And though I opposed the war in Vietnam, I never was much for demonstrations, so the young people didn't want me. In fact, my name became something of a dirty word. The end came, though, in the 1968 election between Nixon and Johnson.

ST. PETER: You voted for the loser?

MR. LIBERAL: Oh, I usually voted for the loser. No, I didn't have anyone to vote for.

ST. PETER: What did you do?

MR. LIBERAL: (*simply*) I died.

ST. PETER: Well, let's see, you ate for the hungry, danced for the crippled, drank for the oppressed and fed a black. Anything else?

MR. LIBERAL: Yes, I felt guilty. I always felt guilty. (*guiltily*) I told you I didn't belong here.

ST. PETER: (*opening the gates*) Enter, please, Mr. Liberal and take your seat on the right of the Heavenly Throne.

MR. LIBERAL: (*amazed*) But I did so little good!

ST. PETER: (*smiling*) True. But you did so little harm.

Being a Stevenson admirer, I was appalled when Kennedy put that archenemy of liberals, Lyndon Johnson, on the ticket, nor was I pleased with his attitude toward Stevenson. I firmly believed in the authenticity of a remark attributed to Kennedy after an eloquent speech Stevenson gave as the ambassador to the United Nations. "Nice guy," the new president was supposed to have said. "No balls."

While perhaps apocryphal, it summed up the difference between the two men and inversely reflected the liberals' attitude toward Kennedy. We saw him, in turn, as cynical, arrogant and all too willing to subscribe to Jesse Unruh's aphorism: "There are times when we must rise above principle." I've long held that more people love Kennedy more fervently today than when he was alive.

That said, I was and am an admirer of Kennedy's humor, his intellect, his poise and, particularly, the way he and virtually all the Kennedys leap through life. They are among those intrepid souls who bound into each day and suck it dry. This is their quality I most envy. For I know I lack the energy and courage to live life, as they do, to its fullest.

I had dinner one night at Hickory Hill, Ethel Kennedy's home outside Washington. As the taxi rolled up the driveway, I was delighted by the signs "Don't Even THINK of Parking Here" and "Trespassers Will Be Eaten." Inside the white, wooden, three-story house that rambled over a hill was bedlam. Dogs were leaping for a platter of lamb chops on the table. Joe Kennedy Jr., a forceful, confident young man, was orating loudly about this or that as his siblings laughed, tussled and shouted. Ethel Kennedy is an attractive woman with the Kennedy verve and charm of whom I'm very fond. She was her usual engaging self, but I had the feeling I was in a den of hyperactive exotic animals who were accustomed to casual observers and went about their play while ignoring them.

Over in a corner seated on the floor with his back against the wall was a slender young man quietly smoking a cigarette. This was David Kennedy, the fourth of Ethel's eleven children. I joined him, and we talked about writing and writers. I felt that I had met at least one kindred soul. Six months later, he was found dead. Officials would say only that there were "significant amounts" of drugs in his body.

I never really knew either Jack or Bobby Kennedy, although I followed their campaigns and attended their press conferences and interviewed them briefly. I had a long chat with Ted Kennedy during his brother's 1960 campaign. He had been dispatched ("exiled," some said) to California to direct, theoretically, the electioneering in the West. Local Democrats paid him little heed, referring to him as "the dumb Kennedy." His academic record was a disaster, and his personal life could later be summed up in a single word, "Chappaquiddick." Today, he strikes me as an intelligent, principled, hard-working senator and a devoted family man.

He has, of course, greatly matured, but one thing served to radically change my impression of him. That was a letter he sent me in 1975. At the time, he was manfully forswearing any presidential ambitions. So I wrote a column dated in the future—January 30, 1997—which began "Edward M. (Teddy) Kennedy, kicking and screaming, was dragged up the steps of the Capitol today and inaugurated the 39th President of the United States."

This imaginary account suggested that the Democrats, appalled by the tired politicians seeking the nomination, drafted a reluctant Kennedy, who then conducted a vigorous campaign against his own election, citing Chappaquiddick and declaring he was unfit for the office. Some voters were impressed by his honesty, others felt he deserved what he didn't want, and he won in a landslide. The column ended with Kennedy on the steps of the Capitol turning to the microphones, beaming into the television cameras and delivering the shortest inaugural address in American history: "It worked."

Unfortunately, I didn't keep the letter that Kennedy wrote in response, but the gist sticks vividly in my memory. It consisted of two paragraphs that went something like this:

> That column was the most unfair, scurrilous and unprincipled piece of garbage ever to appear in a respectable newspaper. You should be ashamed of yourself for printing such claptrap.
>
> Besides, it didn't work in 1968, it didn't work in 1972 and I see no reason why it will work next year.

How could you help but not admire a politician who would sign a letter like that?

While Ethel Kennedy is the only member of the clan I knew, I feel I have considerable insight into the Kennedy spirit. This is because one of my dearest friends is Paul B. (Red) Fay, who has been aptly described as more Kennedy than the Kennedys. At 77, he beats me handily at tennis and golf, climbs mountains faster, knows more important people, makes friends more easily and is far, far busier than I. He lives more than any other person I know.

Fay's thinning hair has turned from red to gray, but his blue eyes are as piercing as ever, and his solid body moves quickly, always with a sense of purpose. He comes from a well-to-do San Francisco Irish-Catholic family. He was something of a hellion at Stanford before joining the navy in World War II. As captain of a PT boat in the South Pacific, he met Jack Kennedy, became one of his closest friends and served in his administration as his undersecretary of the navy. Fay's book, *The Pleasure of His Company*, written after Kennedy's death, was not only a bestseller, but was praised by the family as presenting the most accurate portrait of Kennedy as a human being. Needless to say, the portrait was favorable. Today, Fay serves on a dozen boards of directors, belongs to a dozen clubs and inveigles senators and cabinet members to address the seminars he gives annually in Washington and Palm Springs for his corporate clients. In between, we travel together.

Fay is a marvelous traveling companion. We usually travel with four or five other couples, all of them tennis players. Fay is the unquestioned leader. In his briefcase, which used to bear the seal of the undersecretary of the navy until the leather finally fell apart, he carries a yellow legal pad on which each afternoon he sets down the seating arrangement for dinner. At lunch he sits us more informally. I remember one young woman saying to me of a morning. "I love the adventure of breakfast—open seating."

Fay also announces each day's agenda: "All right, gang, at 10 A.M. the Rhodes will play the Kellys on court three—eight-game pro set, no add," he will say, consulting the schedule he has made out. "On court four..."

I constitutionally detest authority, and I initially resented Fay's dictatorial approach, but I soon came to realize that democracy doesn't travel well, and, without Fay, we'd all be sitting around saying: "Well, what do you want to do?" "I don't know; what do you want to do?" Besides, he dealt with the rare objections with his awesome Irish charm, and our days were filled to overflowing.

I've been constantly amazed at his ability to persuade strangers—gate guards, maitre d's, those at the heads of lines—to see things his way. Once, we were staying at a hotel atop a hill in Majorca. All the tennis courts were taken, but Fay spied one next to a home in the valley down below. "There's one that's empty," said Fay, and off we and our dear wives traipsed in our tennis attire down the hill and across the fields. As we approached the large, rambling house a ferocious-looking dog began barking. I manfully volunteered to guard our wives while Fay went up to the door. In a few minutes, he motioned us to come join him in the foyer where Fay introduced me, as was his custom, as "the famous American columnist." Our new warm friends, Senor and Senora Whatstheirnames, said that of course Mr. Fay and his guests could use their court. But what impressed me most was that after we'd played a few games, a butler rolled out a tea cart bearing ice, glasses and assorted beverages. "Isn't it nice," said Fay, pouring himself an orange juice, "to be among people who appreciate greatness?"

I'm ashamed to say that Fay's powers of persuasion also work on me. When we approached Beijing on a Lindblad trip to China, Fay cooked up a scheme whereby I would deliver a lecture on the breeding and raising of Peking ducks to our fellow travelers, most of whom were widows celebrating their husbands' passing. ("Herbert always dreamed of coming to China, so I'm doing it for him.") Together, Fay and I worked out a story line, which began with the ducks mating only at the very apogee of the full moon. Much against my better judgment, I rose to give my little talk. I knew I was in trouble when I reached the part where amahs armed with bamboo rods prodded the little ducklings around a jogging track to take off unwanted fat. I could see Fay in one corner, his back to me, his shoulders shaking convulsively. Between him and me were the seated widows, their lips unsmiling, their eyes fixed on me attentively. My God, they believed every word I was saying! Well, the only thing people hate worse than being hoaxed is the con artist who hoaxes them. Suffice it to say, that I spent the rest of that trip tipping my hat, offering my hand, pulling back chairs, lugging suitcases and otherwise behaving as obsequiously as humanly possible.

In many ways, the stories I love to tell about Fay are similar to the ones he loves to tell about President Kennedy. Fay worshipped Kennedy for his intelligence as much as anything else. But what I treasure about both men is their ability to quicken my blood, to make me see life as a challenge, not a chore.

This was the spirit that permeated the Kennedy years. The nation seemed more alive, the issues more worthy of the fray. We knew then that we could make a perfect world, one where all people would be equal. So my friends marched in Selma and were attacked by Bull Connor's police dogs in Birmingham. (Seeing the dogs were leashed to the wrists of the officers, I still feel that the demonstrators overlooked a simple tactic I offered at the time that could have radically altered the outcome: Uncaging one female police dog in heat.)

I marched only in Washington. While others there that day remember Martin Luther King's "I Have a Dream" speech from the Lincoln Memorial, my more vivid memory was of interviewing an elderly black woman, Mrs. Coralee Persman, who had come by bus from Biloxi, Mississippi. She suddenly interrupted the flow of our conversation. "You know," she said, "this is the first time in my life anyone ever called me 'Mrs. Persman.' That's the kind of remark that makes us liberals feel good.

I also wrote half a hundred columns happily attacking southern segregationists. This one was my favorite:

Act One

Scene: *A magnolia-scented path leading to a pearly gate. Colonel Jefferson Lee Stonewall approaches, nervously fanning himself with his Panama hat. Waiting to greet him is The Gatekeeper who wears a khaki uniform, a badge and a white helmet.*

THE GATEKEEPER: (*smiling*) Now don't you fret none, Colonel. You're not going to have any trouble getting in here.

THE COLONEL: (*with annoyance*) That problem, sir, didn't so much as flicker across my mind. Why, I've been a decent Southern Christian gentleman all my born days. Went to my

Southern Christian Church every Sunday, and, like the Bible says, I loved all my fellow men—excepting, of course, for outside agitators, Republicans and uppity Nigras.

THE GATEKEEPER: Of course.

THE COLONEL: (*mopping his brow*) But, tell the truth, I'm a mite worried about what kind of folks you all got inside this place.

THE GATEKEEPER: What kind of folks?

THE COLONEL: (*hesitantly*) Well, I'm not criticizing, mind you, but the Bible's just a trifle hazy on the point. It keeps saying all us decent Christian folks are going to dwell together throughout eternity, but it don't precisely spell our what kind of folks.

THE GATEKEEPER: You mean?

THE COLONEL: (*in a rush*) I mean am I going to have to dwell throughout eternity with a bunch of Nigras?

THE GATEKEEPER: (*shocked*) Why, Colonel, whatever put such an idea in your head? You know they never were allowed in your many fine Southern Christian churches. You think for one minute they're going to be allowed in here?

THE COLONEL: (*with an immense sigh of relief*) Praise the Lord. Who, as we used to say in church, never would have created separate races if he didn't believe in segregation.

THE GATEKEEPER: That's right, Colonel. It's the way you reckoned it ought to be. You just walk in through those pearly gates marked "White Only," and the colored folk, they got their own separate-but-almost-equal facilities down over there across the tracks. No intermingling. You'll never see a Nigra again.

THE COLONEL: (*happily*) I knew it all the time. Only you ought to find some way of letting folks know back on Earth. It sure would ease a lot of nagging worries.

THE GATEKEEPER: (*smiling*) They just got to have faith.

ACT TWO

Scene: A magnolia-scented pink cloud six weeks later. The Colonel sits in a wicker chair, sipping moodily on a mint nectar as The Gatekeeper passes by.

THE GATEKEEPER: Enjoying yourself, Colonel?

THE COLONEL: Tell the truth, I'm not. Oh, there's plenty of everything. But there's nobody to serve it with a respectful smile. There's nobody sitting on the back of the cloud. When I holler "Boy!" nobody comes. How can a man feel naturally superior when there's nobody to feel superior to?

THE GATEKEEPER: Well, like I said, there's no Nigras here.

THE COLONEL: You mean, I got to go through all eternity feeling like this? (*snorting*) And you call this Heaven!

THE GATEKEEPER: (*surprised*) Heaven? But, Colonel, I thought you knew . . .

Chapter Six

Love Everybody (Except Penguins)

For close to half a century, my government dragooned me and my fellow citizens into fighting the Communists. It was the most costly war in human history. Our side alone spent more than two trillion dollars on an arsenal of weapons fit to blow the Communists off the face of the earth. And the only Communist I ever knew well was Jessica (Decca) Mitford. A more unlikely enemy couldn't be invented.

Decca, is, of course, one of the "madcap Mitford sisters," the daughters of the Baron of Redesdale, and she must grow tired of reading references to her sister Nancy, the famous novelist, her sister Unity, who was linked with Adolph Hitler, and her sister Diana, a prominent member of the Cliveden set. In a fine act of rebellion, she herself became a Communist, lost her husband, Esmond Romilly, who was killed in World War II, emigrated to the States and married Robert Treuhaft, a dark, saturnine left-wing lawyer with a wry sense of humor. A beauty in her youth, Decca Mitford is now plumpish, gray-haired and bespectacled. She still speaks in that softly slurred, sometimes impenetrable accent of the British aristocracy. Coupled with her vague gestures and sly chuckle, she often gives the impression of a kindly grandmother poised on the edge of her dotage, but she has a keen mind, a sharp wit and a relentless curiosity. Her skills as a writer and an investigator are well attested to by her muckraking books, such as *The American Way of Death*.

I never knew she was a Communist until one evening in the '50s. It was at the height of the McCarthy era, when the hint that a person was, or had ever been, a member of the Communist Party was enough to have the suspect fired, blackballed and ostracized by one and by all. Mitford and I were chatting at a dinner party. To make conversation, I idly asked her whether she was an American citizen.

"Oh, yes," she said. "You see, I had to."

"Had to?"

"To be sure," she said. "You see, when I arrived in this country, I naturally marched straight down to the American Communist Party headquarters to sign up in order to continue the good fight and all that. However, they said I couldn't possibly join unless I was an American citizen."

Ever since that evening, I've found the concept that the American Communist Party posed a threat to take over the country absolutely hilarious.

When I began column writing in 1960, the spirit of McCarthyism was still very much alive. One of its manifestations was Dr. Fred Schwarz, an Australian preacher, who was then the chief purveyor of anti-Communism in this country. The good doctor had founded something he called the Christian Anti-Communist Crusade, which never sounded very Christian to me. Such was his brief eminence that the publisher of *Life* magazine publicly apologized for calling him "hysterical." I felt I could do no less, as I had described him similarly. The magazine, of course, meant running-around-in-circles hysterical. I meant rolling-in-the-aisles hysterical. But I said I hadn't realized that Dr. Schwarz was in possession of the Kremlin's secret "blueprint for the United States," which he announced he was now unveiling for all his followers. In my apology, I had a fine time imagining how Khruschev reacted on discovering that the secret blueprint was missing from the Kremlin's safe:

> "Gone!" cries Khrushchev, leaping to his feet. "In two Ukranian words, *Im Possible*! That fiendish Capitalist master spy Schwarz has outwitted us again. What a disaster! How can we build a Communist America without our Blueprint? Let's see ... (*He sketches furiously*) We were going to attach the Aleutians to Key West with five-eighths-inch bolts, reconstruct Goldwater and ... (*He throws his pencil down*) It's no use. I can't remember how many nuts there are in Southern California."

And so forth. Ah, what a young smartass I was. There's no other word for it. Thus, having apologized to Dr. Schwarz, I announced that I was going into competition with him. If he could make a bundle with his Christian Anti-Communist Crusade, there was no reason I couldn't turn a tidy sum with a crusade of my own. Being new to the crusade business, I naively said that what the public wanted was not another hate crusade, but a love crusade. With great fanfare, I therefore proudly launched the Love Everybody Crusade. It sank like a rock.

Friends said it was a nice idea and all that, but ... After giving the matter a great deal of thought, I decided the truth of the matter is that no one wants to belong to an organization that doesn't exclude someone else. It's the major purpose of organizations. So I raised the Love Everybody Crusade, pumped it dry and re-christened it the Love Everybody (Except Antarcticans) Crusade. As crusades go, it was an overnight smash.

I chose Antarcticans because I felt they wouldn't mind too much serving as hate objects, most of them being penguins. I predicted that the right wing would love hating penguins because penguins were materialistic atheists, or, at best, agnostics. Alien penguins had clearly infiltrated our State Department in large numbers, as anyone who had ever attended a formal State Department banquet would attest. If it walks like a penguin and if it talks like a penguin and if it looks like a penguin, I say it is a penguin.

White supremacists, who were riding high in those days, would fall all over themselves to hate penguins, I predicted, for penguins are not only predominantly black, but their brain capacity is only one-eighth that of a white supremacist. Thus hating penguins would make white supremacists feel sixteen times more superior than they had heretofore. As for the left wing, penguins not only opposed big government, but they were notoriously non-intellectual. Few had any interest in the class struggle. More heinous, penguins were the very symbols of bloated capitalists.

Thousands of readers sent in for membership cards and lapel buttons. I rather liked the buttons. Each bore the legend "Love Everybody (Except Antarcticans)" over a depiction of an innocent-looking penguin with a knife protruding from its back. For three years I wrote frequent columns warning the nation about the penguin menace. Kind readers sent in photographs of penguins, paintings of penguins, statues of penguins, news stories about penguins and several volumes of Anatole France's *Penguin Island*. After three years of this, I disbanded the crusade. I found I had come to hate penguins.

During the course of my crusade, I had noted in various ways that more Americans had seen a live penguin than had seen a live Communist. The dearth of Communists in this country was a serious impediment to patriotic Communist hunting. Many American communities had two, even three Communist-hunting organizations and no Communists to hunt. But while the concept behind McCarthyism was patently ridiculous, its endangerment of our civil liberties and its effects on the careers and reputations of many Americans were, of course, disastrous. I'm proud to say that the CIA began keeping a dossier on me not long after I began column writing. I later obtained a copy under the Freedom of Information Act and was disappointed to find that the majority of entries were snippets from my column sent in by an eagle-eyed patriot over in Oakland. To indicate how McCarthyism operated, here is one typical snippet: Communist Party leader Gus Hall is "sort of lovable."

This was taken from an interview with Hall in which I also wrote "I think Communism is a pretty atrocious idea. And I figured if you could love a Communist, you could love anybody"—the only point being that you could hate ideas without hating those who held them.

I confess to having had some difficulty loving the professional anti-Communists. For the most part, they were a spiteful, humorless lot. One I had a soft spot for, though, was Raymond Hoiles, publisher of the Freedom papers, a right-wing chain of dailies and weeklies. On a swing through Southern California, I interviewed Hoiles in his office in Santa Ana. He was a fine old gentleman who was not only opposed to the draft, but wanted to abolish public schools, public libraries and most other functions of government. Taxes, he felt, were extortion. "If someone takes your money by threat of force," he said, banging his palm on his desk, "that's extortion!"

Now, there was a man to appeal to my anarchist leanings. So I popped by Knott's Berry Farm, to ask its proprietor, Walter Knott, a leading anti-Communist crusader, what he thought of Hoiles. "Oh, he's a fine man and a patriotic American," said Knott, and then, after a moment's hesitation, he added, "Of course, he's something of an idealist."

I certainly couldn't bring myself to hate the few American Communists I've met. Rather, I've tended to feel sorry for them.* Most struck me as highly idealistic and forsworn to the cause of helping the unfortunate. But in this, the richest and perhaps the most content country in the world, their prospects seemed nil, and I wondered what drove them to dedicate their lives to a hopeless endeavor. We had one woman reporter back in the '50s and '60s, the wise and intellectually elegant Carolyn Anspacher. I remember her saying she had a female cousin who was a Communist, "but," said Miss Anspacher, "she had thick ankles."

My feelings about Communism itself, on the other hand, were mixed. When the cold war finally ended with capitalism's triumph, I was in some measure saddened. In theory at least, Communism was based on love and brotherhood: "From each according to his abilities; to each according to his needs." Capitalism, on the other hand, appealed solely to greed: Human beings will work harder if there's more in it for them. So basically this victory was a triumph of greed over love. That greed works and love doesn't is a depressing commentary on the human condition.

Communism in practice, however, is another kettle of unappetizing fish. My political bible ever since I was a teenager has been George Orwell's 1984. With the rise of fascism in the '30s and Communism in the '40s and '50s, his vision of the future seemed to me so increasingly possible that I was, and still am, frightened by any form of totalitarianism. In any totalitarian country—the Soviet Union, Cuba, East Germany, Haiti—I have always tended to panic, worrying irrationally about how I was going to get out. Conversely, while I am a milquetoast in most of my dealings with my fellow human beings, I am a veritable tiger if my rights are defied at an intersection or if some poor building inspector suggests entering my home without a warrant.

---

*With the outstanding exception of aforementioned Decca Mitford, let me quickly add, whom I envy and admire for the rich and fulfilling life she's led.

As the cold war progressed, more and more of the Orwellian future seemed to unfold. I was particularly fascinated by the ease with which the powers that be could manipulate our fear and emotions. In *1984*, you may recall, the story is set in Oceana, which is constantly at war with either Eurasia or Eastasia. One fine scene describes a Hate Week rally. The crowd is being driven into a frenzy of rage against the fiendish forces of that despicable enemy, Eurasia. In the midst of all this invective, the rabble-rousing orator is handed a slip of paper telling him that the enemy is no longer Eurasia, but Eastasia. "In mid-sentence, not only without a pause, but without even breaking syntax," Orwell tells us, the speaker shifts his attack on the fiendish forces that must be destroyed at all costs. Now, however, the despicable enemy is, of course, Eastasia.

In a very real way, this reflected what went on during the cold war. Back in the '70s, I wrote a column about one Daniel Delver, who had a compulsion to be well-informed on world affairs. Unfortunately, shortly before the end of World War II, a pile of *New Republics* along with the Sunday *New York Times* toppled on him. He lapsed into a coma, not to be revived until twenty years had passed. His faithful wife, Evangeline, was at his side, to hear his first words:

"Have we crushed that wily Oriental nation?" asked Delver as his eyelids raised.

"Do you mean Japan or China, dear?" said Mrs. Delver hesitantly.

"Japan, of course," snapped Delver. "China is our ally, staunch and true. I do wish you'd read more."

"Well, things have changed a bit," said Mrs. Delver gently. "Japan's our ally now and China's our enemy. Please, drink your hot milk."

Delver's eyes glazed slightly. "Japan's our ..." he muttered. "Well, what about the Italian front? Are we smiting our ruthless foes hip and ... Why do you look at me like that? The Italians are our enemies, aren't they?"

"Not any more, dear," said Mrs. Delver. "They're our friends. I think you'd better rest now."

"Friends?" said Delver, sitting up. "Good. With

their help, we and our loyal Russian brothers will crush the fiendish Huns like ... What's the matter? Don't tell me the Russians aren't our brothers any more."

"Not exactly." said Mrs. Delver, nervously.

"Well, never mind," said Delver, "with the Italians on our side, we'll still be able to defeat the dirty Boche and ..."

"No, dear," said Mrs. Delver, "we've already defeated the dirty Bo ... the Germans. They're our staunchest allies now. But they're a little perturbed with us at the moment. You see they feel we're not wholeheartedly prepared to go to war in order to save them from the fiendish Russians. Fortunately, though, the fiendish Russians are quarreling with their allies, the awful Chinese, who in turn are casting covetous eyes on our wonderful friends, the Japanese, who ..."

The column ended with Delver lapsing back into a coma, the doctors saying he had lost his will to become well informed and Mrs. Delver concluding he was happier that way. There was some truth in this last, for if the poor man had awakened again in another twenty years he would have found that the impoverished Russians and the striving Chinese were once again our friends while the busy Japanese and efficient Germans were the biggest threats to our economic well-being.

But lucky Orwell. He wrote in those relatively halcyon days before the Cold War. The grim, totalitarian state he envisioned seemed indestructible, yet we readers knew in our hearts that somehow, some day it would be overthrown and its people would get on with the business of advancing the human condition. We readers had hope.

All through the '60s, '70s and '80s, however, we lived under the threat of a nuclear holocaust. During the Cuban missile crisis, I would lie awake consumed by the fear that at any instant hydrogen bombs would tear apart me, my family and the world. It was as real as the fear one feels awaiting a biopsy report. To fear the enslavement of the human race is one thing; to fear its extinction is another.

I tried to capture this in a dozen or more little fables I wrote over the years about the Beautiful Green Valley where the wildflowers grew. The Valley was peopled by the Goodguys who lived in Wonderfulland and the Badguys who dwelled across the river in Awfulland. The Goodguys fervently wished to save the Badguys from Awfulism. With equal dedication, the Badguys were determined to save the Goodguys from Wonderfulism. To achieve these ends, the Wondrous Wizards created awesome beasts known as Psnxtls. These were gifted with poisonous breaths, fiery eyes and insatiable appetites. "But don't worry," said the Leaders of the Goodguys and the Badguys, "we have chained up our Psnxtls so tightly that the world is safe." In each of the fables, of course, the Psnxtls got loose one way or another and ate everybody up. So it was always a happy ending because the Goodguys saved the Badguys from Awfulism, and the Badguys saved the Goodguys from Wonderfulism. True, the wildflowers were none too happy, but that was because they didn't understand geopolitics.

As the '60s rolled on and no bombs fell, we adjusted even to the prospect of Armageddon, proving once again the astounding adaptability of living things. By the middle of the decade, the explosive power of the nuclear weapons we and the Soviets had ready in our arsenals was equivalent to covering the land surface of the planet three feet deep in TNT. Yet, for the most part, we went about our daily lives as though there were no nuclear bombs. Some of us marched in peace rallies or wrote letters to our congressmen, but most of us blithely ignored the fact that we were wading through our mundane daily routines while up to our asses in dynamite.

Even though I constantly wrote about the prospect, I doubted many people believed the human race could come to an end—intellectually maybe, but not in their hearts. Perhaps there would be a nuclear war, God forbid, but our species would somehow survive. Our finite minds are poor mechanisms. They are unable to comprehend either infinity or eternity. Perhaps they are equally incapable of envisioning a world without humans. Or perhaps it's our megalomaniacal conviction that this boundless cosmos with it trillions upon trillions of blazing suns was created solely for us featherless bipeds on this out-of-the-way speck of dust.

That's why I've always liked a column from that era purporting to be an interview with a grumpy dinosaur whose swamp was drying up:

"If you make no attempt to adapt to these changing conditions," I asked him, "aren't you afraid you'll become extinct?"

That drew a snort from him. "Extinct!" he growled. "Are you out of your mind? There have always been dinosaurs and there always will be dinosaurs. After you've been ruling the world for 140 million years, there's one thing you know in your bones."

"What's that?" I asked.

"The Good Lord created this planet," he said, "solely for the enjoyment of dinosaurs."

Of course, today more scientists than not believe the dinosaurs perished with a bang, not a whimper, but no one's yet come forward to challenge the astounding egocentricity of the human race. The other quality that saw us through those nightmarish decades was our unlimited capacity for hope. We are much like that little boy in the fairy tale whose wicked stepmother gave him a room full of manure for Christmas. She returned the next day to find him still manfully shoveling away. "I just know," he explained, "that there's pony in here somewhere."

So we kept on shoveling. The Soviets orbited *Sputnik*, the first man-made object in space. We panicked. Good Lord! If their missile technology was that far ahead of ours, they could probably blow us off the face of the planet in a twinkling. So we desperately speeded up our own space program. In two short months—with great fanfare and with the television cameras rolling—we pressed the red button to launch our own satellite atop a giant Vanguard rocket. The rocket promptly exploded, and the little six-inch ball that represented our aspirations in space went skittering across the tarmac, beeping plaintively.

Adding insult to injury, the Russians sent hero cosmonaut Yuri Gagarin orbiting the planet to become the first human being in space. To show them they couldn't intimidate us, we countered by launching Alan Shepard from Cape Canaveral out into the Atlantic—bang, zip, splash. While my colleagues were jotting down quotes from the brave Mr. Shepard, I interviewed Alberto J. (the Great) Spinelli, widely known as the Human Cannonball.

"I had a great sense of gladness and humility," said Mr. Spinelli after his flight of 68 feet, 11 inches at Bischoff's Big-Top Circus. "It was just like Yuri Gagarin. So the only difference is he goes a little farther."

But I knew we'd never give up—not after I heard on the radio that a chimpanzee had been spotted 100 miles over Savannah, Georgia. Sure enough, it was one of ours! Yes, sir, the hairy little fellow became the first American to successfully orbit the planet. After the landing, the Associated Press rocketed a bulletin from Cape Canaveral hailing this "freckle-faced astrochimp" and the great mission the "intelligent, dead-panned" space voyager had accomplished. I knew then that we had, in our mysterious way, crowned a new national hero. Once again, it proved that the times make the man, or, if the times are desperate, the chimpanzee.

Eventually, of course, we did orbit a human astronaut, John Glenn. At the time, I felt I had caught a glimpse of the tail of that pony. When Yuri Gagarin soared around the planet, it seemed like some cheap parlor trick. We didn't see him take off or land. We were only told about it by those untrustworthy Soviets. It was not that I didn't believe in his feat, it was that I didn't experience it. But when John Glenn's tiny white rocket strained upward toward the stars behind the glass on my television set, my spirits soared with him. He was one of us. Now it was we—he and I—who were taking our first step out from this planet that has nurtured us. It's not much of a planet as planets go, smaller than most. It circles a middling-sized sun on the fringes of a galaxy of 200 billion suns flying outward through a universe of countless other galaxies, some so distant that it takes their starlight ten billion years to reach the lenses of our seeking telescopes.

As I watched Colonel Glenn sail upward, my faith was reinforced. I don't believe in a God who directs my everyday affairs, although I do superstitiously thank Him for his bounty when the occasion arises. But I do believe in an all-encompassing purpose. It's not so much that I believe there is a purpose; it's that I can't believe there isn't. I can't believe we were brought forth on a tiny planet circling a middling-sized sun on the fringes of mediocre galaxy only to die there. I have faith that our destiny lies somewhere out in that starry vastness. I can't justify that faith logically. But then just as logic is the only justification of logic, so faith is the only justification of faith. At last we were on our way to the infinite stars, to the countless galaxies, to the ends of space—to our destiny. By God, we were going to make it after all!

All this stimulated yet another Landlord column. I've written scores of them over the years, all in the same format. While, as I say, I don't believe in a God who bothers with my own, insignificant destiny, I do have a deep fondness for the Landlord.

Scene: The Heavenly Real Estate Office. The Landlord is happily rummaging through his Galaxy Construction Kit while singing, "A couple of jiggers of moonlight, and add a star ..." His business agent, Mr. Gabriel, enters, Golden Trumpet in hand.

THE LANDLORD: Now I know I had a jar of moonlight in here somewhere ...

GABRIEL: Excuse me, Sir, but You really must do something about that little blue-green planet that You love so well.

THE LANDLORD: Earth? Oh, pish and tosh, Gabriel, everything is going according to plan.

GABRIEL: Plan! Good You, Sir, the present tenants have become certifiably undesirable. Not only are they still mucking up the property, but they are now on the verge of blowing up the whole shebang.

THE LANDLORD: (*sighing*) Yes, yes, I know, Gabriel, and I had such high hopes.

GABRIEL: For the likes of them? Really, Sir, they've been quarreling and squabbling and vandalizing ever since You gave them the lease. Honestly, they behave as though they thought they owned the place.

THE LANDLORD: They were merely children, Gabriel.

GABRIEL: And as they've grown older, they've grown worse. Now they not only pollute Your air and Your waters, but they threaten to make the property uninhabitable. (*raising his Golden Trumpet*) By every sound principle of business management, I must sound The Eviction Notice. Ten ... nine ... eight ...

THE LANDLORD: (*holding up his hand*) No need for that,

Gabriel. They are taking The Test.

GABRIEL: The Test, Sir?

THE LANDLORD: Oh, it's quite simple, really. I merely gave them the secret of unlimited energy to see what they would do with it.

GABRIEL: And if they pass?

THE LANDLORD: Why, they will use unlimited energy to eliminate hunger and want and any conceivable reason for nations and wars. Moreover, with unlimited energy they will be able to voyage out among my stars in maturity and brotherhood to achieve my purpose.

GABRIEL: And if they fail?

THE LANDLORD: (*sadly shaking his head*) Then they will evict themselves.

So all through the '60s, '70s and '80s, I had the feeling that I was living through the most critical moments in the history of the human race. In the long nights as we teetered on the razor's edge, I worried that we would fail the Test. Our apartment overlooks San Francisco Bay. On clear nights, I would often sit on the porch taking in the fragility of the city that lay before me. I would watch the headlights of the cars flitting across the Bay Bridge in the far distance. I would watch the blinking lights of planes and helicopters sailing across the black sky like tiny spaceships. A thousand golden streetlights glittered below me. Nearby windows gave forth the blue flickers of television sets. Across the Bay, a twinkling rosy glow climbed the hills. Beneath the lights, a fantastic web of wires and cables and pipes and tubes of electric wires and coaxial cables lay encased in uncountable tons of concrete and asphalt, bricks and steel, binding together the once-naked hills—all the result of myriad lifetimes of labor and thought. Here, then, was the zenith of our civilization, the end product of our 300,000 years on this planet. And it could all be wiped out in three ticks of a nuclear blast. What an incredibly senseless waste!

Yet all through those perilous times, I wrote columns saying that we would somehow muddle through. I didn't say how. I didn't know how. I wrote them mainly to reassure my own worried children, and their tone was one an unarmed father might employ as the hungry tigers circled ever closer. It's hard to remember how much we feared the Soviets' might and how insoluble the conflict seemed. Thanks in part to the initial shock of *Sputnik* and Yuri Gagarin, the Soviet Union appeared at least our equal, if not technologically our superior. In Richard Rovere's excellent biography, *President Kennedy*, he reports that in 1961 the new president was presented with estimates based on CIA figures warning that by the year 2000 the gross national product of the USSR would be triple that of the United States. Now there was an enemy to drive sleep from one's bed.

The sudden collapse of this mighty Evil Empire was stunning. In 1990, my wife and I toured eastern Europe and Russia as the Berlin Wall was coming down. As we wandered through the grim cities and despoiled countryside among the shabby people, we felt no victorious elation. This was the enemy? "They simply put everything they had into military hardware," explained an American expert on Soviet affairs whom I talked to in Moscow. "There was nothing left for anything else."

The tigers had been of paper. We had conquered a Potemkin village. And at what cost!—to ourselves, our children and our children's children. Here's a column about that:

> A spring moon washed the huge concrete monolith in a milky light so soft it seemed almost to heal the webbed cracks of centuries that marred the once-glistening surface of this, The Holy Temple of The Tribe.
>
> The Immortal Guard, youthful priests chosen for their loyalty, fierceness and strength, stood at attention a hundred strong across The Portal, barring entrance to the sanctuary, for the two-foot-thick steel door had long since rusted away.
>
> The High Priest swayed rhythmically below the altar, holding aloft his symbol of office, a jagged stick representing the lightning of heaven. Somewhere in the darkness, drums beat.
>
> Slowly, the Tribe emerged from the tangled jungle to kneel in the clearing below The Temple, for it was once again time for the annual Ceremony of Reassurance and Consecration.

Gradually, the tempo of the drums increased. At the very edge of the clearing, a young member of The Tribe, not older than five, crouched beside his mother.

"Mother," said The Young One. "Mother, I'm afraid."

"Hush," said The Mother. "Hush, now, dear. Everything will be all right."

"Tell me again, Mother," said The Young One. "Tell me what is inside The Temple that we guard so carefully."

"The Holy Dust, dear. The Holy Dust."

"And what is The Holy Dust, Mother?"

"It is the legacy of our Ancestors. They left us The Holy Dust in sacred trust."

"Tell me again, Mother. Tell me about our Ancestors."

"They were like gods, dear. Like gods. They could create lakes and rivers and destroy mountains. They made the night like the day."

"And how did they make these miracles, Mother? How?"

"They captured a creature called The Atom and learned its secrets, such as how to make lightning. And with their lightning, they could do whatever they wished, and they walked the Earth like gods. When they had finished making their lightning all that was left was The Holy Dust. This they have willed to us as their legacy."

"May we see The Holy Dust, Mother? May we?"

"Oh, no! No one may look upon The Holy Dust, for it would burn out their eyes and dissolve their bones. Its power is beyond comprehension."

"Mother," said The Young One, drawing close, "I'm afraid."

"Hush, now," said The Mother. "There is nothing to fear. For ten thousand years we have guarded The Holy Dust to insure it does no harm. And we will guard it for ten thousand more. That is our legacy."

The Young One shuddered. "But, Mother, if it should escape . . ."

"Fear not, dear. Everything will be all right. Listen! Listen to The High Priest."

The drums fell silent. The High Priest poised motionless for a long, dramatic moment. Slowly, he intoned in a sing-song voice The Creed of Reassurance and Consecration—a creed that had been recited each spring by a High Priest for ten thousand years:

"There is no cause for alarm. A safe method of disposal will soon be found. Meanwhile, if we guard carefully the contents of these containers, they can do no damage to any living creature. Fear not, everything will be all right."

As one, the members of The Tribe sighed with relief. They then lifted their pointed snouts to the stars to give thanks to their Ancestors for their legacy as the light of the gibbous moon danced on their silvery scales.

Chapter Seven

To Root against Your Country

Vietnam. How many times I have typed those three syllables. They still ring darkly in the jungles of my mind. Those three syllables cleaved the nation more decisively than any issue since the Civil War. They set hawk against dove, rich against poor and parents against children. They exposed the clay feet of our revered leaders, tore apart our faith in our government and cast a noxious pall that hangs over our republic even yet.

At first, I confess, I treated Vietnam lightly. President Kennedy —worried about his defeats at the Bay of Pigs and in Laos and frightened by Khrushchev's bluster—was determined to show how tough he could be, so he began beefing up the South Vietnamese army. To me, it sounded like a tempest in a teapot, and when he began dispatching military advisors to Saigon, I suggested they were prepared to engage the enemy in "hand-to-hand advice."

But by 1964, the devastation of that poor little country by American air power had begun. To comment satirically on the looming disaster, I invented the tiny Asian nation of West Vhtnnng. As I now like to boast, if it hadn't been for the more than 300 columns I wrote on Vhtnnng and Vietnam during the ensuing eleven years, we might well have become bogged down in a land war in Asia.

Each of the Vhtnnng columns began the same way: "It was in the 43rd year of our lightning campaign to wipe out the dread Viet-Narian guerrillas ..." Despite the growing seriousness of the war, I took a somewhat juvenile delight in the indigenous names. West Vhtnnng was ruled by General Hoo Dat Opp Dar, who was constantly being overthrown by General Hoo Dat Don Dar. Other characters I loved were the buxom beauty queen, Hao Bot Diem; the recalcitrant guerrilla leader, Kris Ma Phut; the obsequious vice president, Dat Sma Boi; the director of military planning, Wat Nao; the fleeing premier, Pak Opp Ngo; and the evil plotter, Nho Diem Ghud. The capital of the country was, of course, Sag On, and the crucial hamlets for which mighty battles raged included Cao Dng, Wat Pho and War Dat.

The first Vhtnnng column appeared in March of 1964 following talk in Washington of invading North Vietnam on the theory, I presumed, that if you can't lick 'em, go lick somebody else. In the column, our secretary of defense was making his monthly "crisis mission" to West Vhtnnng to propose "a bold dramatic step" to General Hoo.

"Surrender?" suggested the general hopefully.

"Never!" said our secretary firmly. "We cannot afford to lose West Vhtnnng, not to mention California, Illinois and both Dakotas in the fall election. No, the Loyal Royal Army must launch a do-or-die invasion of the impenetrable stronghold of East Vhtnnng."

"What are you," inquired General Hoo politely, "some kind of nut?"

"The alternative, as I see it," said our secretary imperturbably, "is to redouble our effort here in West Vhtnnng. Our 15,000 military advisors will drop twice as many napalm bombs. We'll make twice as many strafing runs. Bomb! Burn! Destroy! Destroy! With luck, we'll blacken every square inch of West Vhtnnng. Blood will flow in ..."

"Blood?" said General Hoo. And he fainted dead away.

In that same vein, I envisioned what victory would mean, particularly to our geopolitical goals in Southeast Asia. The scene is a flag-draped rostrum in the capital of Sag On where, after 15 years of bombing, our officials are saluting the entire surviving population of Vhtnnng. His name is Mr. Thang Sa Lot. Asked to say a few words of appreciation, Mr. Thang surveys the smoking ruins of his country, thinks for a moment and at last speaks up. "With America as an ally," he says, "who fears Communism?"

I wrote a number of serious columns on the subject. Here's one from 1973:

It is Memorial Day. Across the land, politicians will stand on flag-draped rostrums paying tribute to the nation's war dead.

What will they say about the 58,000 young Americans killed in Vietnam? What can you say? What can you honestly say?

"We are gathered here today to honor those 58,000 young Americans who gave their lives ..."

That's a lie. With the exception of kamikaze pilots and the like, no soldier gives his life. He risks it. If he loses, it's taken from him—bitterly against his will.

"... in a glorious cause ..."

That's a lie. In the beginning, so long ago, some Americans may have thought Vietnam was a glorious cause. But now we are sick unto death with the whole bloody business. Yet young Americans are still dying there.

"... heroes all ..."

That's a lie. Few soldiers are heroes. Most in Vietnam were draftees. It was the Army or jail. Vietnam or the stockade. Fight or be court-martialed. They died because we forced them to die.

"... for the good of their country..."

That's a lie. This war has alienated our young, all but destroyed our economy, eroded our faith in our leaders and created a miasma of doubt and hopelessness that has poisoned our land.

Yet what can you say? This is all we can honestly say?

*

We are gathered here today to tell those 58,000 young Americans how terribly, terribly sorry we are.

You died because of our pride and stupidity. You died because we compounded error on error. You died because we couldn't bear to be humiliated by a tiny, backward nation.

You died because our leaders, like all leaders, are fascinated by the game of geopolitics. You died because they mistakenly thought that by moving a few of you there in the beginning, like pieces on a board, they could counter the enemy's advance.

You died because our generals said that if they only had a thousand more pieces, a hundred thousand more pieces, five hundred thousand more pieces, they could checkmate the enemy forever.

You died because our bureaucrats, like all bureaucrats, gave our leaders only rosy reports about lights at the ends of tunnels. You died because our leaders feared that if they admitted defeat, the voters would rise against them. You died partly because of their national pride and partly (this is the hardest to bear) for domestic political considerations.

You died because the human mind found it impossible to think of each of you as a living being with hopes and hang-ups and desires, good and bad. You died because our leaders thought of you as a troop. And in death you became a "casualty figure." They did worry about you then.

To be honest, these are the reasons you died. And we are terribly, terribly sorry.

In a more satiric vein, the other characters I used repeatedly for the next decade were Private Oliver Drab and Captain Buck Ace. Drab, 374-18-4454, was, of course, the stereotypical grunt. When his draft board announced he would have the privilege of serving in his country's uniform, he said he would like to be a mailman. They then gave him his choice of stemming the tide of Communism in Southeast Asia or going to jail. He often regretted his decision. The format of these columns was invariably the same:

Captain Ace, all spit and polish, would give a command, and Drab would question it. The captain, usually in a fatherly fashion, would explain the military necessity of the order. Then, under Drab's naive inquiries, he would grow increasingly testy until he exploded. Afterward, Drab would review the argument with his friend, Corporal Partz.* Here's an example based on an actual news story, the capture and subsequent abandonment of Hill 875 by the 173d Airborne:

> "I see where we moved off Hill 875," said Corporal Partz, reading from a newspaper on his lap as he cleaned the toenails of his right foot with a trench knife.
>
> "Which one's that?" his friend, Private Oliver Drab, 378-18-4454, asked without much interest. "They all look alike to me."
>
> "What!" snapped Captain Buck Ace, for he had overheard, and his military mustache was quivering. "You mean to say, soldier, that you've forgotten Hill 875 so soon?"
>
> "Was that the kind of pointy one, sir, where we liberated a couple of chickens?" said Private Drab hopefully as he scrambled to his feet and saluted. "I remember that one."
>
> "For your information, Drab," said the Captain coldly, "Hill 875 is where the 173d Airborne wrote one of the most glorious chapters of this war. They captured the summit on Thanksgiving after five days of bloody fighting for every inch of that hallowed ground. And though they took nearly 500 casualties, still they pressed on to the top."
>
> "Oh," said Private Drab. "I wonder why."
>
> "Because it was there," said Captain Ace simply. "It was their job to take it, and they took it. What a proud moment! How would you like to have been one of those survivors who reached the top?"
>
> "Yes, sir, I'd like to have been one of the survivors," said Private Drab, nodding. "But what I mean, sir, is why go to all that trouble to take a hill we don't want. The paper here says that now we've got it, we're giving it up."
>
> "Let's see that," said Captain Ace, grabbing the newspaper. "Well, I think the headquarters spokesman explained

---

* The name Corporal Partz was one of those hidden jokes that some writers delight in. As a few readers guessed, the corporal could never be demoted because "Private Partz" was not acceptible in family newspapers. Ah, those innocent days.

it pretty well. See, he says here, "No hill is that critical to hold forever. There are plenty of hills in that area."

"Oh, said Private Drab again. "Then why didn't we take one of those others?"

"Because the enemy wasn't holding them," explained the Captain patiently. "We wanted Hill 875 because the enemy had fortified it. Now they fortified because they knew we'd want it. So it was costly to take it. But now that the enemy is no longer holding it, naturally we don't want it. Thus once we had it, military strategy dictated that we give it up. After all, it's no good to us."

"Yes, sir, but if we'd decided in the first place that it was no good to us, we wouldn't have wanted it, and they wouldn't have fortified it, and we wouldn't have . . .'"

"The reason, Drab, that you'll never make a soldier, damn it," said the Captain contemptuously, "is that you just don't have a military mind."

∗

"Well, maybe he's right." Private Drab said after the Captain had stomped away. "But I still don't see this fighting and dying for something you know you don't want."

"You got to look at the big picture, Oliver," said Corporal Partz philosophically. "Hill 875 is a symbol."

"You mean because it was a famous victory?"

"Nope, I mean what goes for Hill 875," said Corporal Partz, wiping his knife on his pants, "goes for this whole lousy country."

The major issue in these columns was what on earth Drab was fighting for. The reasons given by our leaders kept changing. Initially, Captain Ace explained that Drab was there to advise the Vietnamese. Drab's advice, needless to say, was that everyone should put their guns down and go home. Next, he was told he was fighting to preserve South Vietnam's democratic way of life. But as one dictator followed another, this wore thin. (In Vhtnnng, our soldiers were ordered to "get out there and die for General Hoo.") Then, as the tides of battle turned against us, it was decided that we were fighting for peace. This puzzled Drab because we weren't technically at war with anyone, but he felt it was the best cause he had heard of yet. In a conversation with Corporal Partz, however, he decided that "way down deep, what I'm really fighting for every day is to stay alive." Partz agreed, "but," he said, "it ain't no cause to die for."

Vietnam. What monstrous, ugly, foolish butchery. Three million Vietnamese and 58,000 Americans died because of the pig-headed egocentricity of our leaders. I rarely write a serious column. I don't know enough to be a pundit. So when I abandon satire, it is only when I feel deeply moved enough to report on my own emotions. It took me a long time, but finally I grew sufficiently angry to write a serious column expressing my feelings of betrayal. It appeared in March of 1971:

> The radio this morning said the Allied invasion of Laos had bogged down. Without thinking, I nodded and said, "Good."
>
> And having said it, I realized the bitter truth: Now I root against my own country.
>
> This is how far we have descended in this hated and endless war. This is the nadir I have reached in this winter of my discontent. This is how close I border on treason:
>
> Now I root against my own country.
>
> How frighteningly sad this is. My generation was raised to love our country, and we loved it unthinkingly. We licked Hitler and Tojo and Mussolini. Those were our shining hours. Those were our days of faith.
>
> They were evil; we were good. They told lies; we spoke the truth. Our cause was just, our purposes noble, and in victory we were magnanimous. What a wonderful country we were! I loved it so.
>
> But now, having slogged down the tortuous, lying, brutalizing years of this bloody war, I have come to the dank and lightless bottom of the well: I have come to root against the country that once I blindly loved.
>
> I can rationalize it. I can say that if the invasion of

Laos succeeds, the chimera of victory will dance once again before our eyes—leading us once again into more years of mindless slaughter. Thus I can say I hope the invasion fails.

But it is more than that. It is that I have come to hate my country's role in Vietnam.

I hate the massacres, the body counts, the free-fire zones, the napalming of civilians, the poisoning of rice crops. I hate being part of My Lai. I hate the fact that we have now dropped more explosives on these scrawny Asian peasants than we did on all our enemies in World War II.

And I hate my leaders, who, over the years, have conscripted our young men and sent them there to kill or be killed in a senseless cause simply because they can find no honorable way out—no honorable way out for them.

I don't root for the enemy. I doubt if they are any better than we are. I don't give a damn who wins the war. But because I hate what my country is doing in Vietnam, I emotionally and often irrationally hope that it fails.

It is a terrible thing to root against your own country. If I were alone, it wouldn't matter. But I don't think I am alone. I think many Americans must feel these same sickening emotions I feel. I think they share my guilt. I think they share my rage. If this is true, we must end this war now—in defeat, if necessary. We must end it because all of Southeast Asia is not worth the hatred, shame, guilt and rage that is tearing America apart. We must end it not for those among our young who have come to hate America, but for those who somehow manage to love it still.

I doubt that I can ever again love my country in that unthinking way I did when I was young. Perhaps this is a good thing.

But I would hope the day will come when I can once again believe what my country says and once again approve of what it does. I want to have faith once again in

the justness of my country's causes and the nobleness of
its ideals.

What I want so very much is to be able once again to
root for my own, my native land.

I wrote the column in one of those foolhardy I-don't-care-
what-they-do-to-me moods. I wasn't sure whether the *Chronicle*
would print it. A number of papers across the country didn't. One
editor, Reg Murphy of the *Atlanta Constitution*, felt so strongly on
the subject that he sent me a letter of apology for not running it. It
might pass muster in San Francisco, he said, but not in the South. I
waited nervously for the mail. In he end, I received eighteen letters
calling me a Benedict Arnold or worse, but close to 2,000 readers
wrote to say they agreed with my feelings. Never, before or since,
have I received so much mail on a column. I still hated the war. But I
felt a whole lot better about the country.

Chapter Eight

NOBODY FOR PRESIDENT

I've always subscribed to the theory that newspaper people should be observers, not participants. For one thing, it's a noble excuse to avoid speaking, auctioning or judging snail races for this cause or that. In this business, you are often asked if your columns have any effect on public policy. I answer, half seriously, that I hope not. Who wants to be responsible for the mess we're in?

The other questions that constantly crop up are:

Q: Where do your get your ideas?

A: I read through the paper until I find an item I don't understand. Then I sit down at the typewriter and explain it to everybody.

Q: How long do you spend writing your column?

A: It used to take eight hours, but I took a speed typing course and now I can knock one out in twenty minutes.

Q: (invariably from a college student) How much money do you make?

A: None of your business.

Q: Are you a liberal?

I hate that one. In the long-ago Adlai Stevenson days, I was a diehard liberal, but as the years passed and my knowledge of politicians and the workings of bureaucracy grew, my faith in governmental solutions weakened. My social contract is that I agree to join the tribe so that it will defend me from saber-toothed tigers, other tribes or the fellow in the next cave who might, if it were not for tribal law, bop me on the head. The sole function of government, then, is to protect me from others, whether they be muggers, foreign enemies or corporate polluters. I am thus opposed to compulsory Social Security, withholding taxes, motorcycle helmet laws or any other legislation designed to protect me from my own shortcomings.

Nor, of course, am I any great believer in the promises of politicians. When Lyndon Johnson ran against Barry Goldwater in 1964, I introduced a new candidate, Nobody. In all modesty, the Nobody for President campaign touched a public chord. I gave out several thousand red-white-and-blue Nobody for President buttons and wrote dozens of columns extolling Nobody's virtues.

The columns were set in Nobody for President headquarters, where the pompon girls, known as Nobody's Sweethearts, sang the campaign theme song, "Nobody Loves You." The candidate would then expound on the issues of the day, such as Vietnam. "We should simply withdraw all our troops and declare that we won," Nobody said.* The columns would usually end with this fearless leader delivering a rhetorical question to his devoted followers, such as, "And whom can you trust to keep his campaign promises?" Oh, how the rafters would ring with the name of the candidate!

A major reason for my distrust of politicians was the way they were forced to raise campaign funds. Lobbyists, of course, have long denied they bought a legislator's vote. All they bought, they claimed, was "access" to explain their point of view. "And what did you get for the $10,000 you contributed to Congressman Boodle?" a corporation president might be asked at a stockholders' meeting. If he righteously replied, "Absolutely nothing," he should be given a small golden parachute and heaved out the window.

Here's a still timely column on the subject that dates back to 1971. Those involved are Walter Cronkite, Roger Mudd and Eric Sevareid:

> "Good evening. Well, another Auction Day has rolled around, and here in Auction Central we'll be bringing you the results as long as any races are still in doubt. I think we already have a few scattered bids. Let's go down on the

* This strategy was later advanced by Senator Aiken of Vermont and certainly superior to the final outcome in which we withdrew our troops and declared we'd lost.

floor and find out. Are you there, Roger?"

"Right, Walter. Actually, we don't have too much to go on yet. Nothing that would indicate a trend. The Democrats have come up with a bid of $10 million for the presidency, but, of course, that's just to get the ball rolling."

"Right, Roger. Anything on any of the local races around the nation?"

"No, Walter. Wait, here's a flash. The Democrats have just conceded the mayor's office in Philadelphia to the Republicans for a high bid of $247,643.17"

"Thank you, Roger. I think we were rather expecting a Republican victory there, weren't we, Eric?"

"Yes, Walter. The basic strategy of the Democrats in Pennsylvania has long been to concede Philadelphia and save their campaign funds to buy the governorship."

"'Buy the governorship' You know, Eric, I may be an aging fogy, but I can't help thinking the old election system was better than this out-and-out buying of public offices."

"What's the difference, Walter?"

"Oh, I know the arguments, Eric. Back in the '60s and early '70s virtually every election was won by the candidate with the most money. And yet ..."

"You have to remember where the money went, Walter. It was spent on press agents, billboards, television commercials, bumper strips—a total waste. Now, of course, local, state and federal governments will probably take in more than $3 billion on today's Auctions. It's a boon to the taxpayer."

"I'll grant you that, but ... What is it, Roger?"

"Sorry to interrupt, Walter, but George Wallace has just bid $32 million for the White House. It looks as though he's got some Texas money behind him this year and is going to make a real three-way race out of it."

"Thank you, Roger. As I was saying, Eric, I can see where political parties prefer the new system. Imagine spending $32 million on a losing campaign and having nothing to show for it. This way, losing doesn't cost you a nickel. But for the man on the street ..."

"I think you've forgotten how bored your man on the street became once he realized the richest candidate would win. We've just spared him six months of tee-vee spots, junk mail and ugly billboards."

"Yes, I suppose. But it's too bad the parties couldn't agree on fair laws to limit campaign spending so that the best man would have a chance of winning."

"It's too bad horses can't fly, Walter."

"Well, I ... What is it, Roger?"

"I thought you'd want to know, Walter. The Newark City Hall's just been bought for $182,642.17."

"By the Republicans or the Democrats, Roger?"

"By the Mafia, Walter."

"Thank you, Roger. Well, I'm glad some things don't change. Right, Eric?"

"At least the money will go to lower taxes, Walter. Don't forget the slogan behind Auction Day—'As long as the politicians insist on buying public office, let them buy them from the public.'"

I had another thought about buying elections when the incredibly wealthy Texas oil man Michael Huffington was halfway through his 1994 campaign against Dianne Feinstein for senator from California:

Michael Huffington, who was worth $70 million before he got into politics, was at the door, soliciting funds for his Senate campaign.

"You want *me* to give *you* ten bucks?" I asked.

"Yes," he said, "your support will help me resolve the major question this nation faces today, which is how to get rid of that lying, thieving, rotten Dianne Feinstein and her God-awful hairdo."

"I'm glad you're facing up to the issues," I said, "but, to tell the truth, I'm kind of partial to Dianne. After all, she's worth only $22 million, so I can't help thinking of her as the candidate of us poor folks."

"You won't feel that way after you hear my bold and daring program for radical campaign reform," he said.

"Everybody agrees that's what the country needs," I said. "Everybody but the campaigners. How will your reform work?"

"Well, up to now, I've spent $10 million of my own money on 30-second spots and the like in order to buy the five million votes I'll need to win the election."

"That's $2 a voter," I said. "Poor Dianne, she's only spent about $1.50."

"Shows you how little she values your vote," he said contemptuously. "What's more, I've pledged to spend whatever it takes from here on in to buy more than she does."

"Even $6 a vote?" I said. "By golly, you may set a record."

"Thank you," he said. "But listen to my reform plan: Instead of throwing away that $6 on 30-second spots, I'm going to give it directly to you, cash on the barrel head. Got change for a ten?"

"You think I'd sell my precious heritage for a $6 mess of pottage?" I said indignantly.

"OK," he said, "what about $12.50?"

While he was peeling off the money, I couldn't help but compliment him on his faith in human nature. "It so happens I'm an honest voter," I said, "which is one who, when bought, will stay bought. But what about the others? Once they close the curtains on that voting booth, can you trust them to keep the promises they made you during the campaign?"

"You're right," he said with scowl. "You voters are a devious, greedy, irresponsible lot who are in this political game only for the money."

"But once they see the unbounded faith you have in us American people, I'm sure they will turn over a new leaf," I said, holding out my hand.

"Well," he said, stuffing his money in his pocket, "back to the old 30-second spots."

But the truth is that I'm more interested in writing than politics. My drive is megalomania, not power. I once had a discussion with Paul Jacobs about this. Jacobs was a left-wing labor agitator who came later in life to write prolifically against a myriad of social injustices. I, on the other hand, was a writer who came later in life to politics. If we both wrote powerful pieces that caused an orphan's life to be saved, Jacobs would be proud of saving that life. I, to the contrary, would be proud of the powerfulness of the piece.

My rising anger at the Vietnam War, however, sullied the purity of my treasured objectivity. I became so worked up that I actually took part in a peace march with a dozen other *Chronicle* colleagues. To show that we hadn't lost our detachment, we carried a six-foot-long banner, retrieved from someone's basement, which read, "Welcome General De Gaulle," that being the only banner we could find. As we approached the rally in Golden Gate Park, we were stopped and interviewed by a reporter from Agence France Presse. I've often wondered whether the news that a group of San Franciscans had heard the French were about to revenge Dien Bien Phu by rejoining the fighting in Vietnam made the pages of *Le Monde*.

It was not only the deceit and patent stupidity of the Vietnam War that appalled me. As a dyed-in-the-wool civil libertarian, I felt the attendant draft was the most massive government assault on individual freedom imaginable. Whether a cause is worth fighting and dying for should be determined solely by those who are to do the fighting and dying. Any other course requires unforgivable egocentricity and callousness. I wrote scores and scores of columns attacking the draft from every point I could conceive. I envisioned it as a ravenous monster to whom we threw our children in a sacrificial rite. I wrote a long column joining the national outcry against a proposal to draft our daughters into the horrors of war just so that I could end it with "So we will draft our sons instead." I said that exempting college students was genetically sound, for by selecting those who were too poor or too stupid to go to college and sending them off to be killed, we were well on our way to wiping out poverty and stupidity. I envisioned a young man who went down to his draft board and eagerly requested to be sent to Vietnam. "I want to go over there and kill those Commies," he cried. "Kill! Kill! Kill!" He was rejected, of course, as mentally unstable.

Needless to say, my columns against the draft endeared me to college students. To me, these young rebels seemed more against the draft than the war, and, when the draft finally ended, so did most campus unrest. But they wholeheartedly agreed with my attacks on both, and thus was I tugged into the college lecture circuit. I loathed every minute of it. It's one thing to express an outrageous opinion from behind the safety of a typewriter. The death threats arrive in harmless envelopes. It's another to stand nakedly before row upon row of your grim-faced judges and struggle for their approbation. If that wasn't enough, I came to feel like a whore. I spent weeks writing the best speech I possibly could. I then delivered it time and time again. I would alter a few paragraphs here and there to keep up with the current political jokes, but, as it was the best I could do, there was no point in writing a different one. So, like Nixon talking about his mother's pies, I would tell the same anecdote over and over again, repeat the same gestures, smile the same smiles and frown the same serious frowns. I hated it when these tired devices manipulated the audience to laugh or turn solemn; I hated it even more when they didn't. Nor did I care for the attendant fuss made by the local arrangements committee. Here's a paraphrase of the standard response that the late humorist Harry Golden made when asked what he charged for a lecture: "My fee is $1,500. If you don't meet me at the airport, it's $1,250. If you don't invite me to dinner beforehand, it's $1,000. If there are no coffee and cookies afterward, it's $750. If you don't drive me back to the airport, I'll do it for $500." My sentiments precisely.

Even thirty years later, I can deliver that speech virtually word for word. I would start by expressing my thanks for the introduction. I would explain that I was grateful for any introduction after my recent experience in Orange County, a hotbed of right-wing activism, where a kindly woman had introduced me as a "nationally syndicated Communist." There wasn't a grain of truth in that line. I had stolen it from a fellow columnist, Adeline Daley, but it served to establish my important credentials.

Being a specialist in nothing, I had to talk about everything. The device I employed to open that can of worms was birth control. At the time, Paul Ehrlich's best-seller, *The Population Bomb*, was convincing readers that they were all about to suffocate each other. I was philosophically opposed to population control. To me, it smacked of elitism. We were saying that life is a private club, and we were not about to spoil it by admitting too many members, particularly black, brown and yellow ones. Nor was I impressed by the argument that we were preventing unwanted children from being born for their sake. This struck me as particularly specious. Virtually everything that's alive struggles to remain alive no matter how pain-filled its life may be. Sentient beings have the choice of ending theirs whenever they wish, but even the lowliest starving, crippled, diseased Calcutta beggar rarely does. That we should make this decision for them in advance struck me as indefensibly overweening. So I employed the satirical device of extrapolation, which operates on the theory that any proposed course of action, if extended far enough, can be made to look patently ridiculous. Thus I would tell the audience, "Birth control may be able to solve *some* of the problems of the human race, but only total birth control can solve *all* the problems of the human race—and in a single generation, too."

This, of course, allowed me to spell out the problems total birth control would eliminate, all of which I had already detailed in old columns. I would then wind up the speech each time with: "So ban the mom! Think of generations yet unborn and let's keep them that way. To save the world it is up to each of us to do his or her part and practice birth control. Indeed, as you look each day on the seemingly insoluble problems you face, what better advice could you seek than to get out there and practice, practice, practice."

For an hour or so of this, I was generally paid the princely sum of $1,000—two weeks' pay in those pre-inflation days. But after five years of it, my dear wife made me give it up, bless her, and I have been a happier, if poorer, man ever since.

Though I loathed the lecture circuit, it did keep me in touch with the younger generation. The older of my own four children were just beginning college, and it helped to know what they faced. On a sunny morning in May of 1969, I was scheduled to speak at the University of California at Berkeley. My second daughter asked to come along as she was unsure whether she wished to enroll at UC in the fall. I parked my old Karman-Ghia convertible on Telegraph Avenue just outside Sather Gate a few hundred yards from Sproul Hall, where I was to appear. During my talk, I heard a few extraneous noises, but none too distracting. When my daughter and I came out, however, Telegraph Avenue was all but deserted and a blue haze hung in the air. By the time we reached my car, our eyes were streaming from the tear gas, for this was the morning of the People's Park riot, in which one student was killed, seventy were injured and hundreds were arrested. As we drove off, my daughter turned to me with a big smile, her cheeks shining wetly, "Oh, Daddy," she said, "I'm going to love Cal."

Chapter Nine

. . . .

SEX, DRUGS AND TREASON

Of all the factors involved, I sometimes think sex was the most forceful in ripping open the generation gap. With the advent of the Pill, sex came out of the closet where my generation had neatly tucked it, and we didn't like its looks one bit. As a civil libertarian, I of course opposed censorship in any form, for I was a tolerant sophisticate who could take sex or leave it alone. How well I recall giving my second daughter the requisite paternal lecture on sex education. "And so," I concluded after twenty minutes of graphic details delivered in a calm, rational, academic manner, "sex is a normal bodily function no different than eating or breathing."

"How often do you and Mommy do it?" she asked.

"Mind your own business," I explained.

That was still the attitude I carried into a panel discussion on obscenity at the outset of the sexual revolution. I and two liberal academics of my vintage were to analyze that beast one evening at Mills College, a somewhat elite private institution for women in Oakland. The three of us nattered on about how obscenity was in the eye of the beholder and should be viewed as a social lapse at worst. Then we came to the question period. The young women wanted to know what was wrong with the word—and even now I must steel myself to type it—"fuck." Well, we discussed its Anglo-Saxon origins and its pejorative nature in great detail while these well-bred young women flung it about for a good half hour, but none of us three old fogies was ever able to say it out loud in their presence. It was then that I realized we had a generation gap on our hands.

To be sure it was "the word that won the war," but only in all-male company. It was the word that Norman Mailer cleverly disguised as "fug" in his *The Naked and the Dead*, inspiring Tallulah Bankhead to say, on being introduced to him, "Oh, yes, you're the young man who can't spell "fuck." And it was the word that got Lenore Kandel, San Francisco's "love poetess," busted in the early '60s before we all became enlightened. I was called by the defense to testify as an expert witness at her trial, for I'd written a column on the Anglo-Saxon Love Poetess who was pilloried in A.D. 872 for employing the ancient Druid word "xptl" in one of her love poems. I took the stand, gave my name and occupation, and the judge looked down on me to inquire, "And exactly what is it you are an expert in?" I was dismissed.

The liberated young women at Mills College who were so free with four-letter words had replaced the "silent generation" of young mossbacks whose ambition during the Eisenhower years was to get good grades at a good college so they could get a good job at a good firm with a good retirement plan. Conservatives, of course, didn't much care for this sea change. This new generation of students, thundered right-wing politician Max Rafferty, were majoring in "sex, drugs and treason." To help him out, I had my fictitious daughter, Malphasia, a column regular, write home to say she had aced sex and drugs, but wasn't doing too well in treason. Yet Rafferty, on the whole, was right.

Once the younger generation had freed itself from sexual taboos, it seemed there was little else to talk about. And what a boon to humorists. For say what you will about sex, it's basically hilarious. The foreplay's inane, and the positions are ridiculous. Yet we spend billions of dollars, trillions of energy ergs and immeasurable Machiavellian devices to achieve a momentary blood rush — a sensation not unlike that induced by an amyl nitrite popper.

Over the years, I've catalogued my columns. In checking the files, I find that close to 500 of them are on the subject of sex. They begin, innocently enough, with the concept of a coin-operated chastity belt. The device, I wrote, would be equipped with jaws that operated on the principle of a parking meter, thus discouraging violations. Its purpose, of course, was to enable the government to tax our last untaxed activity.

Sexual fads came and went. In 1964, it was wife-swapping. One of my stock column characters, the Kindly Old Philosopher, wanted to swap his wife for a washing machine. In the end, however, he rejected the whole scheme. "You mean to say," he said, "that all you get is another wife?"

By 1966, topless dancers, waitresses and musicians titillated customers, newspaper readers and vice squads. I remember Dick Tuck's remark on viewing an "All-Girl Topless Band" in a North Beach night club. "It was better," Tuck said, "before the accordion player quit."

My research on this fascinating subject took me back to the prehistoric kingdom of Erotocea, where, in 8104 B.C., a female dancer named Karul Dodo showed up for an audition with a bad cold and asked Samm, the nightclub owner, for permission to try out in her muu, a sort of tightly knitted sweater. Her performance was less than a terpsichorean masterpiece, but as Samm watched, a strange light came into his eye.

"You're hired, kid," he said when she'd finished.

"Gee, thanks," she said, "and wait till you see me perform without my muu."

"You do," said Samm, "and you're fired."

The rest is pre-history. Crowds of the curious flocked to see the famed topped dancer. Women sniffed, "What's she got to hide?" but the effect on men was overwhelming. For the discovery unleashed one of the most powerful forces the world has ever known—the male imagination. In his mind, each man saw under Ms. Dodo's muu the female form divine, the one he had always been searching for. And as she never shattered illusions by removing her muu, she drove strong men mad with frustration and desire.

The custom spread. Topped dancers were followed by topped waitresses and topped all-girl bands. Soon even the most respectable ladies were wearing muus and, eventually, muu-muus. Legions of Decency were formed under the slogan "Take It Off." Priests thundered from their pulpits, "If the Lord God Ur had wanted women to hide their bodies, they would have been born with muus on." Said a wise philosopher, "Unless women once again display their charms, mankind will enter a period of decadence, immorality and a snickering preoccupation with sex that could last ten thousand years."

It did.

Wife-swapping and topless dancers were followed by streaking, gynecological photos in *Playboy* and a whole host of sex books, such as *The Joy of Sex*, *Everything You Always Wanted to Know about Sex But Were Afraid to Ask* and *The Sensuous Woman*. This last advised housewives to greet their husbands at the door each night in a different fantasy costume while holding a bowl of whipping cream or, if weight was a problem, Redi-Whip.

At the time, I took comfort from treasured passages in my Bible, such as Genesis 12:15, in which Abraham swaps his wife, Sari, who was "very fair," to the Pharaoh of Egypt in return for "sheep, and oxen and he asses, and menservants, and maidservants, and she asses, and camels," a swap the Kindly Old Philosopher would readily approve. I also treasured Genesis 19. It begins with Lot offering his two virgin daughters to a mob of angry men saying, "Do ye to them as is good in your eyes." But all three escape to a cave, where the older daughter says to the younger, "Come, let us make our father drink wine, and we will lie with him, that we may preserve the seed of our father." And so it ends happily: "Thus were both the daughters of Lot with child by their father." I treasure these passages almost as much as I treasure Numbers 31:8–42. That's where Moses and the Israelites mass rape 32,000 Midianite virgins. No, sir, there's nothing like taking comfort from the Bible when the good Christians start talking about censoring books.

Ah, pornography! I've always defended pornography on the grounds that if the second-hand depiction of an act is depraved and despicable, then the act itself, in the flesh, is clearly even more depraved and despicable—particularly within the bonds of marriage. What can you say to a man or woman who performs a depraved and despicable act on the person he or she has promised to love and cherish? If the one's a misdemeanor, the other should be a felony.

I heard another defense from a pornographer. I've long belonged to a Writers' Round Table, to which we members bring distinguished literary guests. The only guest I ever brought was a pornographer. He was a short, round, sleazy-looking man with a tiny mustache. I sat next to him at lunch, and, as none of my colleagues would speak to him, I learned much about writing pornography. First, he wanted it known that he had written more books—forty and more at last count—than anyone else at the table; that each had sold like hotcakes; and that therefore he had more readers than anyone else in the room. His technique, he said, was simple: He spent a day or two writing each book. Then he would go back and insert six or seven pornographic scenes. At this point, he waved a hand that encompassed the dedicated writers around the table who had spent their lives struggling for success. "Hey," he said, "it's a snap!"

I asked him if he didn't worry that his works would lead to rapine and pillage. "Look," he said, "a good porno book doesn't only stimulate the sex urge, it satisfies it."

In the '60s and '70s, it seemed as though we were awash in sex. I wasn't surprised to read that the human race was performing one hundred million sex acts a day, several of them presumably aimed at procreation. I said it was no wonder cigarette sales were increasing, which allowed me to be the first to publish, or so I claim, the World's Funniest Joke. As everyone knows, this goes:

"Do you smoke after intercourse?"
"I don't know; I've never looked."

In any event, so liberated had sex become that the Pope was forced to announce that taking pleasure from it, within marriage, of course, was not a sin, for sex was fun, or so he'd heard. "So," said Mrs. Hennesy, mother of seven, on hearing the good news, "now he tells me?"

At the same time, the Church and its allies were embarking on their long public fight against abortion. It was a wrath-stirring issue. As for me, I faced it foursquare and took the liberal cop-out: As an opponent of the death penalty, wars and population control, I was a firm right-to-lifer. On the other hand, as a believer in individual freedom at all costs, I strongly supported a woman's right to control her own womb. In the end, I took the latter stand.

Besides, I was appalled by the way our lawmakers knuckled under to the right-to-lifers and denied abortions to the poor. With

Roe v. Wade, abortions became as legal as tonsillectomies, yet here was the right wing on the one hand decrying these welfare mothers who had strings of illegitimate babies allegedly to increase their government checks and on the other hand denying them abortions. Ah, well, to paraphrase Abraham Lincoln, our lawmakers must love the poor, or they wouldn't create so many of them.

Moreover, while I try to extol the sanctity of life while spreading mustard on my hamburger, I have mixed feelings about its embryonic stages. A viable fetus is one thing, a clump of a dozen cells is another. When does human life begin?* The Pope said it was at the instant the tiny little spermatozoa finally wriggled its way into the relatively large, hairy egg. Pow! The miracle of human life! It wasn't that this microscopic two-celled creature was to be treasured for itself, my right-to-life friends explained, it was to be treasured for its potential.

All well and good, but what about the potential imbued in the sperm and egg before they mated? Naturally, I identified with the sperm. If a fertilized egg is entitled to his or her constitutional rights, what about the little fellow who did the fertilizing? Surely every spermatozoan is magnificently alive, definitely human and, in this country, unquestionably American. It is true that their numbers are legion, their life expectancy all too brief and their mission virtually impossible. Yet their dedication, their determination and their indomitable grit should be held aloft to our young people as an example of Americanism at its finest.

To comprehend the incredible challenges these countrymen of ours face, let's take a typical spermatozoan I'll call Harold. For his first ninety days, Harold lolls about, growing and gathering his strength. Then, looking like a cuddly tadpole, he is deemed ready for his quest. With 80 million or so of his fellows, he gamely charges

---

* I have always felt that a deep philosophical truth was revealed by the story of a PBS debate on this very subject between a Catholic priest, an Episcopalian minister and a Jewish rabbi. The priest argued that the magic moment was at conception. The minister was willing to compromise on the second trimester. After going hot and heavy, they finally turned to the rabbi to ask when he thought life begins. "Life begins," said the rabbi, pulling thoughtfully on his beard, "when the children leave home and the dog dies."

forth to seek the egg, who has descended from her ovarian bower to demurely hide in the folds of the fallopian tube, where she will await a swain. His little tail flailing away, Harold manfully struggles onward ever onward as, one by one, to the left and right of him, his companions collapse from exhaustion. At last, he and he alone of the 80 million, wins through to his soulmate. They are joined, and Harold, if the right-to-lifers get their way, finally earns his constitutional rights as an American.

A heartwarming story, but rarely true these days. More likely, Harold and his friends will rebound against an impenetrable barrier until death takes them. Or they may perish in a sea of toxic chemicals. Worse, Harold may somehow win through and part the fallopian folds only to find that, thanks to the Pill, no one's home.

Some masculinists may argue that they have the right to do as they please with their own spermatozoa, but if we are going to pass laws against abortion, surely, for Harold's sake, we'll have to pass laws against birth control, not to mention—not in polite company—the sins of onanism.

Actually, I've long been a crusader for onanism. Once the sexual revolution was in full swing, I began dreaming of a counterrevolution, mainly because I was a happily married man. Initially, I described a new fad, monogamy. Always advocate, I say, what you're stuck with. I'm afraid monogamy didn't catch on except with one swinging young man who wrote to say that he practiced monogamy on the dining room table and thought it was swell. So in the early '70s I began sounding the trumpets for onanism, or, as I was forced to describe it in those more restricted times, "solosexualism."

My protagonist was J. Herbert Narsissis, who married himself in 1973 in Kalamazoo, Ohio. "It seemed kind of queer," said the judge after the brief ceremony in which Narsissis vowed to love, honor and cherish himself until death did him part, "but I couldn't find anything in the law against it."

The happy bridegroom called his unusual marriage "a tremendous breakthrough" for the Sole Lib movement, of which he was the founder, but he did object to the judge's use of the word 'queer.' "We're not gays nor are we straights," he said, "and we're sick and tired of all the blather about both. We prefer to be known as 'soles.'

We enjoy sole food, which is whatever we like, and we purchase nothing but sole clothes, which makes us the only Americans who dress to please ourselves."

On a typical date, Narsissis said, he would ask himself out on the spur of the moment to a sole bar where a one-man or one-woman band in a corner might be playing "Love Alone." After making eye contact in the mirror, he could ask himself to dance without fear of rejection. When the evening was over, he would simply pick himself up and murmur, "My place or mine?" His marriage would suffer none of the little squabbles over picking restaurants, movies or vacation spas. When it came to where to leave the toilet seat, he could leave it anywhere he damn well pleased, and if he forgot his anniversary, he certainly wouldn't get all in a swivel.

I wrote several columns on the subject back then, and none raised an eyebrow. Twenty years later, Ann Landers came right out and extolled masturbation as "a cheap, easy, safe way to do it." I saluted Ms. Landers for her courage and revived solosexualism in her honor. Like her, I received not a few testy letters. It was the word "masturbation" that did it. Obviously, that was J. Herbert Narsissis' sex life, but as long as I didn't go into it no one was offended. And yet I was surprised by the reaction a word could cause in this latter day and age.

In a creative writing class in college back in 1948, I submitted the kind of short story a feisty young realist would write. My professor's comment: "Few magazines will print the word 'bastard,' and none will print the word 'ass.'" How delightfully the times change. Fittingly enough, 1992, the Year of the Woman, was followed in 1993 by the Year of the Penis. Here was a word that had long been employed only scientifically, if at all, in either family newspapers or polite society. But even before Mrs. Bobbitt chopped off Mr. Bobbitt's, respectable journals such as the *Denver Post* and the *San Francisco Chronicle* were celebrating the year by running stories on penile enhancement.

To my mind, this organ is the most ugly appendage affixed to the human body, uglier than the middle toe, the nose or even the ear. I asked several women acquaintances how they would enhance it. Their replies ranged from "Paint a happy face on it" to "What are you, some kind of sick-o?" More helpful was one suggestion that it be made retractable like a turtle's head so that it could be tucked away when unneeded, which is most of the time. Another woman, less practical, thought "it might be fun" if it glowed in the dark.

Seeing that it can't be made to glow in the dark or retract, however, the only conceivable way to enhance it is to make it smaller, not larger. "Small is beautiful," as Governor Jerry Brown used to say. "Less is more"—particularly when it comes to ugliness. A friend suggested that men enhance their brains instead. With bigger brains and smaller penises, perhaps the former would finally come to dominate the latter. Once again, there was angry mail, virtually all of it from men. You wouldn't believe the number of men who wrote to say their penises were beautiful. None, however, offered evidence to substantiate their claim, nor did I ask.

All that was before Mrs. Bobbitt overdid an enhancement operation on Mr. Bobbitt. I hoped at the time she hadn't read my column on the subject. As intriguing as Mrs. Bobbitt's lopping was, the nine-hour surgery two doctors performed to reattach Mr. Bobbitt to his attachment fascinated the public. A woman reader sent me a clipping of the story on which she had scrawled, "What for?" What for, indeed? By all accounts, Mr. Bobbitt was a hard-drinking, macho ex-Marine with a penchant for rough sex. Would he be a better man without his penis? Unquestionably! Wouldn't we all? This is the organ that leads men into wars, fist fights and messy divorces. When it comes to the ills of the population explosion, it clearly shares at least half the blame. Can you imagine Teddy Roosevelt leading the charge up San Juan Hill without a penis? I think not. Would Joey Buttafuoco have lured Amy Fisher into that motel to discuss Red Sox pitching? Don't be silly. And there might always be a throne of England if Prince Charles had only been born unendowed. With artificial insemination available at every corner clinic, penises are no longer necessary. They get in the way of a well-tailored suit, they're constantly squabbling with zippers, and they're prone to itching, as any baseball viewer will tell you. True, eliminating them would reduce the number of women attending the ballet, but it would also eliminate penis envy. (A woman I know once defined penis envy as going camping with a man in the snow.) So I called upon every man who cared a whit about the future of the human race to lay his principles on the chopping block. Ah, well, back to the old drawing board.

How dreary all this makes the issue of prostitution, once one of our most delectable of sins. Seeing that the Supreme Court has upheld the pro-choice contention that a woman has the right to do what she wishes with her own body, I don't see why that doesn't include the right to rent it out. Certainly there is no activity that better sums up what our free enterprise system is all about. In recent years, there has been increasing talk of regulating prostitution, usually at the municipal level. I assume this would require establishing a Sexual Facilitation Agency, staffed by sexual facilitators hired through competitive civil service examinations with, of course, no politically incorrect considerations given to age, sex, weight or other handicaps.

The Sexual Facilitation Facility, itself, will be designed in the style known as Government Modern. This requires pouring a large block of concrete, hollowing it out and sticking an American flag on top. The interior will feature green linoleum floors, bright fluorescent lighting and framed photographs of the mayor and the alderman. The cream-colored walls will be enlivened with red arrows over signs saying "Applicants Line Up Here."

Once in operation, the facility will be open from nine to five, Monday through Friday. Those applying for services will take a number and have a seat in a large waiting room. Once called, the applicant will proceed to one of six windows, two of which will be staffed, except during the lunch hour or coffee breaks. Once the applicant has provided a utility bill or other proof of residence, plus a medical history and a fee for the service requested, he will line up for a supervised shower and again for a physical examination. After being processed by the first available sexual facilitator, he will be interviewed by a trained social worker gathering material for a governmental study on the nuances of sex.

This would seem a fitting end to the sexual revolution. One of the goals of those early battlers for sexual freedom back in the '60s was to demystify sex, to force society to look upon it rationally as a normal human activity, and to a large measure they succeeded. But there was always the danger that we would come to look upon sex as another tiring, sweaty exercise like jogging. Like jogging, it was good for a woman's waistline and bad for her hairdo. Jogging might aerobically benefit a man's heart, but in the end it was boring.

Naturally, I began a crusade to keep sex dirty. Where was the Legion of Decency and the Watch and Ward Society when we needed them? Take sex education out of the schools and put it back in the gutter where it belongs, I said. Only by banning books in Boston, requiring undershirts on male actors and making four-letter words misdemeanors could we restore sex to its rightful place behind locked doors.

Needless to say, here was another failed crusade. The sexual revolution flourished. We males who were too old and/or too married to join in the fray could only gaze down on the naked frolicking of our young people with envy or, if they were our daughters, with horror. I always felt that Armistead Maupin captured the spirit of the revolution best in his *Tales of the City*, that intriguing soap opera about gays and straights in San Francisco in those halcyon days before AIDS.

The emergence of gays from the closet was one of the great benefits of the revolution—for the gays, that is, if not for the sensibilities of middle America. I remember how shocked I was in 1961 when a good friend, Roger Boas, who was running for San Francisco's Board of Supervisors, took out a political ad in the bulletin of the Mattachine Society, a gay organization. Boas, a prominent businessman, was a candidate of the Volunteers for Better Government, the squarest of institutions. I had heard vaguely of the Mattachine Society during the '50s. It was virtually an underground cell and the butt of snickering locker room jokes.

"Are you sure you're doing the right thing?" I asked Boas. "I mean, associating your name with that group?"

He shrugged. "That's where the votes are," he said.

And so they were. He not only won easily, but today gays are one of the most powerful voting blocks in San Francisco. Over the years, I developed the typical civil libertarian's attitude toward gays: I would support to the death their inalienable right to do whatever it was they were doing, and I fervently did not wish to think about whatever it was they did.

I rather enjoyed the nature vs. nurture debate about gays. When Vice President Quayle said he believed that being gay was "the wrong choice one makes," I couldn't wait to point out in all fairness that it was certainly a difficult choice. I could see where a young fellow would be tempted to choose the gay life when he reached puberty. Gays are generally more creative and intellectually stimulating than straights, and as they are not burdened with children, gay partners usually have more disposable income to dispose on high living. Not only do they eat higher off the hog, but, like solosexuals, they can leave the toilet seat in any position they like.

On the other hand, the young man who opts for being gay is going to be teased unmercifully by his high school chums, and he's going to get into a lot of fist fights. When he finally finds "Mr. Right," he won't be able to hold his hand in public, nor will either father kiss the bride. Moreover, the happy couple would be wise not to honeymoon in Singapore, Riyadh or Peoria. Worse, he faces a life of discrimination in jobs, housing and Southern Baptist conventions. He can never hope to be an admiral, a general or even a vice president, not if he comes out of the closet.

No, the heartaches of being gay in a prejudiced society far outweigh the joys, and it's just too darned bad that so many young men aren't mature enough to realize this when they face decision-making time.

While Mr. Quayle didn't mention them, the same holds true for blacks. Why people opt for being black is beyond me. True, black can be beautiful, and there is much to be said for being part of such a rich culture. But being black in a white society is at least as difficult as being gay in a straight society. You're the last hired and the first fired. You're more likely than not to be raised in a ghetto, poorly nourished and poorly educated. Your chances of being shot, stabbed or gassed by the state make you a high insurance risk.

Nor do I understand why at least half the people I know decided to be women. I asked a woman friend about this, and she actually claimed she'd made the right choice. I said she was just putting a brave face on her mistake, but she said, no, being a woman meant she could cry if she wanted to or complain if a car ran over her foot.

"What's more," she said, delivering the clincher, "if I'm lost, I can ask for directions."

All too true, I said, but look at the disadvantages: Women have to put up with lower pay, glass ceilings and deadbeat spouses; they must concern themselves with diets, dyes and D-cups, with PMS, postpartum depression and hot flashes; their paths are bestrewn with such obstacles as Senator Specter, Senator Packwood and the Tailhook syndrome—all of which they must overcome with unequal upper-body strength. No, being a woman just doesn't make sense.

If women can justify to themselves the choice they made, I suppose Somalis, Bosnians and Herzegovinians can, too. But there are some choices that defy all reason. Take Mr. Quayle. I can't for the life of me figure out why on earth anyone would choose to be a congenital idiot.

Like all good things in life that I've missed, the sexual revolution did eventually come to an end, brought down in good measure by AIDS. The Christian zealots among us vied to contend that AIDS was divine retribution on gay men for their unmentionable practices. This argument was interesting for its logical conclusion was that God's chosen people were lesbians. It also revealed a rather spotty divine plan for imposing diseases as a retribution for sin. Why weren't rapists at least visited with a good case of jock itch? And it didn't clearly answer the question common to all cold sufferers, "What have I done to deserve this?"

But the sexual revolution, of course, radically altered our culture. Depending on how you look at it, we have progressed or regressed from innocence or ignorance to a society that is liberated from old taboos or one obsessed with the vulgar. In any event, this revolution drove a wedge between many middle-class parents and their offspring, a statement that will be vigorously supported by many a mother and father whose daughter has returned home to spend a few nights with her live-in boyfriend. "Not in our house!" is a cry that's been heard across the land.

But all in all, I think it was a fine new generation that we faced across the gap. Like all new generations, it blamed the preceding one for its problems, but perhaps with more vigor than most. As the father of four, I confess to becoming slightly testy over the constant repetition of my sins. As is the privilege of columnists, I took the easy way of defending myself by writing a column on the subject:

> Once upon a time, there was a man named Ben Adam, who, like most members of The Older Generation, had little hair and overwhelming guilt feelings.
>
> He also had a son named Irwin, who, like most members of The Younger Generation, had lots of hair and overwhelming contempt for anybody over thirty.
>
> "Man, what a mess your generation made of things," Irwin was fond of saying, several times daily. "Because of your bumbling, we face a society that's racist, militaristic, polluted, overpopulated and terrorized by the hydrogen bomb. Thanks a lot."
>
> "I guess we're just about the worst generation that ever lived," Ben Adam would say, nodding contritely. "I'm sorry, Irwin." And Irwin would shrug and wander off to smoke pot.
>
> Ben Adam couldn't help but feel he was in for a bit of divine wrath for his sins. And he was therefore somewhat shaken on awakening one night to find an Angel at the foot of his bed writing in a Golden Book.
>
> "I have come, Ben Adam," said the Angel, "to grant you one wish."
>
> "Me?" said Ben Adam with surprise. "Why me?"
>
> "You have been selected by The Heavenly Computer as typical of your generation," said the Angel, "and your generation is to be rewarded for its magnificence."
>
> "There must be some mistake," said Ben Adam with a frown. "We've been awful. We created a racist society ..."
>
> "Mankind has always been racist," said the Angel gently. "You were the first to admit it and attempt a remedy."
>
> "And we militarized our democracy. Why, when I was a boy, we only had an Army of 134,000 men."
>
> "You built an Army of four million men in hopes of

bringing freedom and democracy to all the world," said the Angel. "Truly, a noble goal."

"Well, maybe," said Ben Adam. "But you can't deny that we polluted the air and scattered our garbage far and wide."

"That is so," said the Angel. "But the environment is polluted solely because you constructed the most affluent society the world has ever seen."

"I guess that's right," said Ben Adam. "But look at the Population Explosion. Famine and pestilence threaten mankind."

"Only because your generation cured diseases, increased the food supply and thereby lengthened man's life span," said the Angel. "A tremendous achievement."

"But we live in terror of the hydrogen bomb," said Ben Adam gloomily. "What a legacy."

"Only because your generation unlocked the secrets of the atom in its search for wisdom," said the Angel. "What a glorious triumph."

"You really think so?" said Ben Adam, sitting straighter and smiling tentatively.

"Your motives were excellent, your goals ideal, your energies boundless and your achievements tremendous," said the Angel, reading from the Golden Book. "In the annals of mankind, the names of your generation, Ben Adam, lead all the rest. And, therefore, by the authority vested in me, I am empowered to grant you one wish. What shall it be?"

"I wish," Ben Adam, the heavenly-chosen representative of The Older Generation, said with a sigh, "that you'd have a little talk with Irwin."

Chapter Ten

The Saga of Elbie Jay

Lyndon Baines Johnson! As Art Buchwald said of him, "I worship the very quicksand he walks on." He was the only man I ever met who fit that improbable phrase "bigger than life"—bigger physically, with his big torso, big face, big hands, big feet and big stride, and bigger emotionally, with his gargantuan rages and overblown sweetness. In his excellent biography, Richard Cato has painted Johnson as the most conniving, corrupt, ruthless and amoral of politicians. I would agree with that. He was also the most productive president since Franklin Roosevelt and, when he wished, an extraordinarily charming man.

Once he had settled into office, I began work on a soap opera to replace the Just Plain Jack series. This one was a Western called "Heaps of Horse Sense." It featured the rootin'-tootin' Jay family and starred their wily pa, ol' Elbie—ol' Elbie Jay. Elbie was known as "the fastest handshake west of the Pecos" and the top wrangler in Texas, where wrangling was a perfected art form. The folksy family consisted of his lovable wife, Birdie Bird, and their two teenage daughters, Myna Bird and Bye-bye Birdie. Herewith a sample:

> Howdy folks. How y'all? Time for another tee-vee visit with the rootin'-tootin' Jay Family—starrin' ol' Elbie Jay, who always deals from the top of the deck, if'n it's his deck.
>
> As we join up with ol' Elbie tonight, he and his pretty wife, Birdie-Bird, are just a-settin' down to a hand of bridge with the man he loves and trusts above all others, the man

he elevated to the second highest office in the land, that unforgettable fighting moderate, Hubert Horatio Whatshisname. Making the fourth is Mrs. Whatshername.

HUBERT: (*holding Elbie's chair*) Well, well, and how are you feeling tonight, sir?

ELBIE: Always thinking of yourself. Who was it gave you your fame and power? I'm the one who made your name a household word. And don't you forget it, Homer.

HUBERT: It's Hubert, sir.

ELBIE: There you go, always trying to get your name mentioned. And speaking of that, didn't I see your handle in the paper again this morning? That's twice in six months, Herbert.

HUBERT: (*blanching*) Honest sir, it was an accident— a traffic accident. I ran over a little old lady, and a reporter with an encyclopedic memory recognized my name.

ELBIE: Well, don't let it happen again. There's no room for publicity seekers around here. The papers only got so much space. Now, let's see. You shuffle there, Birdie-Bird. That's it. Shuffle them good. And you cut, Higbert. That's right. Cut 'em a couple of times. And I'll deal. Hmmmm. I reckon I'll take these thirteen cards here, and you folks can divvy up the rest, fair an' square.

HUBERT: I'm certainly happy with that deal, sir. Would you care to bid now?

ELBIE: Seven no-trump.

HUBERT: Gosh, what a brilliant bid, sir, and I haven't even seen your hand.

MRS. WHATSHERNAME: I'm afraid I'll have to doub . . . Ouch!

HUBERT: She passes too, sir.

ELBIE: A fine woman. You may all be seated now. And I'll just lead this little ol' king of hearts here . . .

HUBERT: A marvelous lead, sir. I'll just have to play my little old three of hearts . . . Whoops!

ELBIE: (*thunderstruck*) You played the ace!

HUBERT: (*pale and trembling*) Honest, sir, it was an

accident. I strategically planned to eat it later when you weren't looking. I reached for the three, but my hands were all sweaty and ...

  ELBIE: Another accident? Hmmm. I always said, Hirschel, that your eyes were set mighty close together.

  HUBERT: (*pleading*) Oh, please don't say you no longer trust me, sir. I'll kill myself.

  ELBIE: What? And get your name in the papers again? Hobart, you're nothin' but a publicity hound dog.

  Can Hubert find happiness in humble obscurity? If he knows what's good for him. Tune in to our next episode, folks. And meantime, as you mosey down the trail of life, remember what Elbie's granddaddy used to say: "Happy is the humble man who don't expect a great deal. But he ain't near as happy as the dealer."

  In all, I turned out seventy-five columns over the years featuring the Elbie Jay character. Most of them ended with a quote from Elbie's ol' Granddaddy. Here's a sampling:

  What is a man profited who gains the whole world. If'n he don't get good press notices?

       *

  Go down unto the people and clasp even the poorest stranger by the hand. He may be a registered voter.

       *

A man with a good woman will go far. But a man with two teenaged daughters will go farther. First chance he gets.

       *

  When you lose friends in politics, lose 'em good.

       *

  Always appeal to a man's better judgment—if'n nothing else works.

       *

  There's nothin' like having young 'uns to comfort a man in his declinin' years. Or to get him there quicker.

       *

Through your good works you become renowned. And through your public works, re-elected.

*

Talk is cheap. So use plenty of it.

*

Ain't no use for proud daddies to worry about their tads marryin' beneath them. They got no other choice.

*

Always fight the good fight—that being one where the outcome ain't in doubt.

*

There ain't nothin' more important in life than trust.
So get all you can.

*

You can always profit from your own mistakes. But it's a sight easier to profit from someone else's.

*

Never marry for money. Marry for love. But make certain sure the feller you love is rich.

*

It matters little whether you win or lose. It's who keeps score.

*

'Tis far better to give than to receive—considerin' what most folks are willin' to give.

*

(On his autobiography, *One Nation Under Me.*) To be known as a great man, you got to make history—so hire a good ghost-writer to do it.

*

Never complain about your lot in life—less'n other folks got their eye on it.

*

When a feller needs a friend, who needs him?

I was proud of these aphorisms. I felt they captured the man's wiliness and egomania. It was the only side of him I saw in Washington and on the campaign trail. I had followed him in '60 and again in '64, when he had the good fortune to run against Barry Goldwater. Now there was a good, decent man with an honest conservative platform. Naturally, he was murdered by us ace reporters. When the billboards went up for the Arizona senator proclaiming that "in your heart, you know he's right," Dick Tuck was the first to append "... of Atilla the Hun"—much to the amusement of us on the press bus. As for me, I parodied the Superman format to create "Gary Boldwater, Boy American!"

Theme: "The Stars and Stripes Forever."

Faster than a Social Security check, stronger than the Chase National Bank, able to leap over tall issues in a single bound, it's Gary Boldwater, Boy American!

So c'mon, kids, let's join Gary Boldwater today for "The Thrilling Adventure of the Phony Treaty." There he is in his disguise as a stuffy old senator wearing his stuffy old horn-rimmed glasses and stuffy old double-breasted suit. That's his pretty secretary, Lotus Lane, who doesn't know his secret identity. She's handing him a document.

Lotus: Here's a copy of that nuclear test ban treaty, Senator Boldwater. Shall I read it to you?

Gary: (*who always pretends he can't read*) Well, now, Miss Lane, I don't see much sense in that. The way I hear, it's just another simple old treaty. Nothing to get het up about.

Lotus: (*vexed*) But, Senator, look: It's written in two languages.

Gary: Now, now, Miss Lane, heaps of thing are written in two languages. Like ... well, like heaps of things.

Lotus: (*angrily*) Oh, Senator, you're just like so many Americans. You're sweet, but you're so naive.

(*She stomps out and Gary whips off his stuffy old glasses and stuffy old suit to reveal the uniform of a general in the United States Air Force Reserve—the uniform of ...* Gary Boldwater, Boy American! *Leaping into the cockpit of his very own jet plane, he zooms into the sky and circles over the Washington Monument.*)

Gary: There! Flying in circles allows me to bring into action my 100 I.Q. brain. Could Lotus be correct? Wait! I shall scan this document with my 20-20 vision. "The governments of ..."

Hmmm. "... discontinuance of all test explosions ..."
Hmmmmmm. "In witness whereof the undersigned ..."
Leaping lizards! Lotus was right! Our nation is in peril!
Oh, that I shall but be in time to save the day!

(*We shift to the Capitol, where our beaming senators are about to ratify the treaty. Suddenly, through the skylight, crashes a parachutist. Could it be? Yes, it is!* GARY BOLDWATER, BOY AMERICAN!)

GARY: Gentlemen, before voting, you should know that among the signatures on this pact is that of one "Andrei Gromyko," a proven card-carrying member of the Communist Party!

(*There are shocked cries of "Oh, no!" and "Egad, sir, he's right!" The treaty is torn up. The senators give Gary a Big Six, before he can modestly slip away. Later, once again in his stuffy old disguise, Gary greets a breathless Lotus Lane in his office.*)

LOTUS: (*glowingly*) Oh, Senator, I wish you'd been there to see him. If only you could be more like that.

GARY: (*winking into the camera*) Well, Lotus, I guess we can't all be GARY BOLDWATER, BOY AMERICAN! (*turning serious*) But it sure would be a great country if we could.

Senator Goldwater was a fine candidate from a satirist's point of view, but he couldn't rival Lyndon Johnson as a target. I suppose I subconsciously resented Johnson for replacing Kennedy. I know I loathed his growing involvement in Vietnam, and I was appalled by tales of his boorish bullying. I gave him little credit for his accomplishments on the domestic scene, and they were legion, particularly in the field of civil rights. I have a somewhat mystic faith that the wisdom of the electorate far exceeds the sum of its parts, including me. The voters knew that Roosevelt was the man for the Depression and the World War II years, and that Truman would find greatness in the dangerous postwar era. While I voted for Adlai Stevenson, they rightly sensed that the nation needed eight years of rest and recuperation under Eisenhower. Time to get the country moving forward again? Who better than Kennedy? As for Johnson, no one but this manipulative southerner could have forced civil rights legislation past the conservative Republicans and Dixie Democrats in the Senate. This was in an era when southern rednecks were defending their rights by bombing black churches, shooting civil rights workers, beating blacks sitting in at lunch counters and attacking black marchers with police dogs. No president did more for blacks than Lyndon Johnson, but at the time I was not about to forgive him for his pig-headed policy in Vietnam nor his Machiavellian egocentricity at home.

Of course, I had seen Lyndon Johnson only in his political milieu. Then, in December of 1966, I spent a week in Austin while Johnson vacationed at his ranch. This was the dry, rolling west Texas hill country where he'd been born and raised. It's a country wooded with scrub oak and pecans, rich in game, where the people are warm with each other and wary of strangers. This is where his roots went deep, and he seemed to me a different man, gentler and relaxed.

This is not to say that the gloriously egocentric Johnson didn't make an appearance. In midweek, he grew bored. Mrs. Johnson was still in Washington, his two daughters were also away and he was by himself at the ranch. So he decided to inspect a half-finished dam that Mexico and the United States had been jointly building across the Rio Grande for the past several years—primarily because it was handy.

To accomplish this required huge fleets of helicopters, buses, cars, trucks and jets from Mexico City, Austin, Dallas and Washington to converge on the tiny Mexican border town of Ciudad Acuna. Once there, the president stood happily erect in the back of an open car to parade through the narrow streets in a light drizzle. Delighted Mexicans shouted "Honson! Honson! Honson!" from the sidewalks, while well-painted ladies in low-cut gowns tossed streamers and confetti from the balconies above. What made the scene particularly vivid were the small children who gathered the soggy streamers from the gutters and let Johnson have it: splat! splat! splat! By the time the parade rounded the final corner past the First & Last Chance Bar, the president was looking more game than happy.

The parade was followed by speeches. At last, Johnson boarded a limousine and set out to inspect the dam, that being the purpose of the trip. The press buses followed, but by the time we caught up, the president had finished his inspection, turned around and headed home.

All of us have a dozen or more days in our lives that we treasure. One of mine was the following Sunday. It was warm and sunny. John

Averill, who covered the White House for the *Los Angeles Times*, suggested we drive the sixty miles out from Austin to Johnson City to observe the president attending church. It was a small, pleasant church with a small, pleasant congregation who paid little attention to the leader of the free world. When the services were over, Averill asked if I would like to meet the president. By that time, I had written more than a hundred columns, in addition to the Elbie Jay ones, attacking him on every ground I could think of. I looked at the way he towered over a few well-wishers in the vestibule, and I actually felt a twinge of physical fear. I screwed up my courage and nodded.

"Pleased to meet you," said the president, grasping my hand in his large one after Averill identified me. There wasn't a flicker of recognition, not a hint of enmity. I was hurt. "You men care to come out and see the ranch?" added the president.

Would we ever? You bet! Only seven of us reporters had bothered to attend the church services. We all piled into our cars to follow the president and his Secret Service cavalcade out to the ranch. The ranch house itself, a rambling, white, two-story building, was surprisingly unprepossessing, yet the president took inordinate pride in it and its surrounding appurtenances, the pride of a man who had built all this from scratch. We trooped through the front door to be greeted by Lady Bird Johnson, who, looking accustomed to spur-of-the-moment invasions, graciously served us coffee and cookies in the warm and—there's no other word for it—cozy living room.

The president was beaming. Would we like a house tour? Yes, sir, Mr. President! He led us from one room to another, pausing here and there to tell delightful, folksy stories about this cowboy painting, that old clock and these fading photographs—the memorabilia of his past. Up the stairs we went and he paused before a closed door. "And this is Luci's bedroom," he said, throwing open the door. And there was Luci, sitting on her bed, fully clothed fortunately, and offering us a somewhat forced smile.

The house tour over, Johnson asked if we might like to see "the burying ground." Yes, sir, Mr. President! Out behind the ranch house beneath a huge oak tree was the family cemetery where his parents and grandparents and other kin were buried in neat rows with two plots reserved for him and Mrs. Johnson. More stories about this uncle, that aunt and the one name I remember, Cousin Oriole.

Would we care to visit "the birthplace?" Yes, sir, Mr. President! Down the lane was a tiny, white, pristine structure, a recently built replica of the farmhouse in which Johnson had been born. As befits a shrine, it was as neat as a pin. The president had filled it with more curios: a crib, a highchair and on the wall a deeply sentimental account of his birth, written by his mother. The president turned on Averill, a tall, bespectacled and very cynical reporter. "Now why don't you just read that out loud for the folks, John?" he asked sweetly.

I swore I could hear Averill's teeth grind, and he manfully read aloud this awful treacle in a rapid monotone. Nevertheless, the president seemed pleased.

And would we care to see the deer? Yes, sir, Mr. President! It wasn't widely publicized—at least I didn't know of it at the time— but the president had fenced in some 200 acres of land out behind his ranch house and stocked it with hundreds of deer, antelope, buffalo and wild turkeys—a sort of private Texas Eden. A bulldozer had scraped winding dirt lanes over the dry, rolling land, and the president dearly loved to drive through this park land, watching the deer and the antelope bounding this way and that.

So the president opened the driver's door of an aging red Mercury station wagon and made the seat assignments. His first pick was Maryanne Means, an extremely attractive correspondent who highly impressed me by wearing two wristwatches—one for the local time and one for her deadline time in Washington. "Maryanne," said the president, "why don't you sit right by me on the front seat?" Maryanne said that would be a pleasure. The president then assigned a male reporter to sit next to her and three more to take the rear seat. That left the bare floorboards in the back for the reporter from *Pravda* and me. Maybe he does know who I am after all, I thought as I climbed over the tailgate.

The president took the wheel, and off we went through the gates in the high Cyclone fence with one Secret Service car preceding us and another following. And there were the deer. What a lovely sight. "Out here," Johnson said softly, "a man doesn't think about missiles."

But as we got closer to the deer, he slowed the car. "You folks better roll up your windows," he said. "It's rutting season, and the deer can get mighty mean in rutting season."

I tried, but the rear window of the station wagon wouldn't roll up, and consequently for the rest of the trip it sucked in dust like a vacuum cleaner.

The car came to a stop. "Let me tell you about rutting season," said the president. "You see those marks on that doe's shoulders over there, Maryanne?"

"Yes sir, Mr. President."

"You see that big buck next to her, Maryanne?"

"Yes, sir, Mr. President."

"Well, Maryanne, that big buck's hooves made those marks on her shoulders."

"Yes, sir, Mr. President."

"What's he mean?" whispered the reporter from *Pravda* impatiently. "What's he mean?"

The reporter from *Pravda* was a short, stocky man with an excellent command of English. Unhappily, he wasn't too good at risqué innuendo, and I spent a good portion of the drive translating the president's remarks for the benefit of readers in the Soviet Union.

After a quarter of an hour observing game, the president had another idea. "Anybody ever see a deer eat a cigarette?" he asked. Well, by golly, it turned out that none of us had. The president picked up the microphone hooked to the dashboard. "Where's Charley?" he snapped. The two Secret Service cars peeled off like dive-bombers. Their mission: Find Charley, the cigarette-eating deer. After a few minutes, our radio crackled. "We've located Charley, Mr. President. He's about 200 yards behind you and to your left."

The president made a skidding U-turn in a handy meadow and bore down on Charley. "Anybody got a cigarette?" he asked. Handed one, he rolled down his window six inches, stuck out the cigarette and ordered: "Charley, come here!"

Well, it being rutting season, Charley had other things on his mind besides cigarettes, and he took off—not down the lane, but smack up a hill strewn with rocks, dead branches and scrub oak. The president, being Lyndon Baines Johnson, followed, one hand on the wheel, one hand sticking out the window and bellowing at the top of his lungs, "Goddamn it, Charley, come here!"

No trail. Just rocks and trees coming at us. "Goddamn it, Charley, come here!" Bang! The back end of the heavily loaded station wagon would hit another rock or rut, and up *Pravda* and I would sail in the unpadded rear. BANG! Bangety-bang-BANG!

The goddamn Charley finally stopped and ate the goddamn cigarette. The president drove the limping station wagon back to the ranch house. *Pravda* and I had to crawl out over the rear seat as the tailgate was thoroughly broken. The president looked at me, bruised and thick with dust, and darned if he didn't smile. "I hope that wasn't too rough a ride," he said politely.

"Oh, no, Mr. President, it was well worth it," I said, and I meant it. What a warm feeling it was to think the president of the United States knew who you were.

One other remark of the president's stuck in my mind. We had all piled out of the car on a hilltop at one point to look at the not-very-impressive view. I was standing by Johnson and said I wanted to thank him for devoting a whole afternoon to showing us reporters around his ranch. "Oh, that's all right," said the president of the United States of America and the leader of the free world, "I didn't have anything else to do."

Chapter Eleven

RICHARD NIXON, NERD AND DORK

When Richard Milhous Nixon died at the age of 81, he had proved once again the adage that any politician can become an elder statesman by living long enough. In the thousands of eulogies extolling his life and works—with the briefly mentioned exception of Watergate—the word "enigma" kept cropping up. The consensus of the pundits is that no one could possibly understand this inordinately complex man. Heck, I did. Dick Nixon was the kid you would never let play unless it was his ball. He was both a nerd and a dork—a highly intelligent nerd and a driving, determined dork—but a nerd and dork nevertheless.

I keep on my desk a photograph of Nixon playing golf. He never played much, but I suppose he wanted to be one of the gang with his rich, golf-playing friends. His was, bar none, the most awkward golf swing I ever saw. His feet are planted in concrete and his elbows are flapping, while his head and shoulders, even though the golf club is pointed skyward, are still hunkered—a word that seemed to be applied only to Nixon. The man, through no fault of his own, simply lacked physical coordination. Yet he went out for football at Whittier College. That he sat on the bench for all those years testifies to both his dorkiness and his determination. How he must have yearned to be one of the team. But it wasn't his ball.

In one of the hundreds of columns I wrote about Nixon, I envisioned in 1970 how different he and the world might have been if he'd been an athlete:

Probably the turning point in Richard M. (Biff) Nixon's fabulous career, as he himself admits, was the day he made the Whittier College football team.

Until then, "that Nixon fellow," as he was known to what few acquaintances he had, was a poor, shy, introverted grind, whose idea of a fun time was an evening in the school library doing crossword puzzles.

His chance came in the third game of the season when the first, second and third string halfbacks broke their legs. "I guess you're all we've got left, Whatsyourname," said the coach with a sigh. "You might as well go in there. It's hopeless anyway."

Well, who will ever forget Biff's dazzling runs of 16, 37 and 98 yards for the touchdowns that beat arch rival Pismo Beach State? That was the first year Biff made All-American.

A grateful alumni rewarded him with a Stutz Bearcat, a raccoon coat and a silver hip flask. Almost overnight, the quiet, studious loner emerged from his dull chrysalis to become the back-slapping, gregarious, whoop-it-up Biff Nixon all America was to come to love and admire.

The column goes on to tell how Biff made the beginnings of his fortune by endorsing Gillette razor blades while playing for the Green Bay Packers and then parlayed his mom's and pop's grocery store into the chain of Biff Burgers that now graces every Main Street in the land. But he never forgot his Quaker upbringing, and thus he came to devote himself to making pacifist speeches and leading demonstrations against the war in Vietnam. Naturally, he had no time for politics and cared little about watching football on television, but he always held a warm spot in his heart for the sport. "After all," he would say, "where would I be today if I hadn't made the team at Whittier?"

A grind? It's pertinent that Nixon finished third in his class at Duke University's law school and that in his three years there he never had a date. Yet he still strove to be accepted as one of the guys, even by the biased press. On that overnight flight to Alaska in the closing days of the '60 campaign, I remember him shuffling in his bathrobe and slippers back to the press section of the plane, where only a few of us were still awake. We were surprised, for he rarely fraternized with us. To me, he seemed ill at ease, his smile forced, as he talked with several of us about football and how hard it was to sleep on airplanes. When he'd returned to his quarters up forward, my seatmate, Robert Novak, announced that this was a historic occasion. "Why's that?" I asked.

"It's the first time since birth," said Novak, "that Nixon has appeared in public without a necktie."

Nixon's penchant for neckties is a puzzlement. He was photographed watering his lawn while wearing a necktie, walking on the beach while wearing a necktie, and awkwardly jumping straight up in the air while wearing not only a necktie but a suit, the jacket of which is carefully buttoned. Yet he still yearned to be accepted as one of the guys. In 1971, at the peak of his power and popularity, he launched what appeared to be a public relations campaign to convince the electorate he was not only a major world leader but down deep just your old buddy from next door:

> "I want you to be perfectly candid about this, Pat. Do you, in your opinion, consider me dull, stuffy or, let the chips fall where they may, not human enough?"
>
> "I have always thought of you, Dick, as human."
>
> "Thank you, Pat, for your confidence. For more than a month now my aides have attempted to project a new image of me, emphasizing the warmly human qualities that make me, in my judgment, a regular fellow, one of the boys."
>
> "Was it difficult, Dick?"
>
> "I did not take the easy path for that is not, rightly or wrongly, my way. I appeared on *The Today Show* to prove I was a regular fellow. I granted countless interviews during which, though I sat in a straight-backed chair, I crossed my legs to show I was one of the guys. And to illustrate my warmly human qualities, I allowed the photographers to take my picture while I was strolling on the beach in casual attire."

"Yes, Dick, I had never seen a more informal photograph of you—wearing that windbreaker with the presidential seal and only a hint of your sincere blue necktie showing."

"I even considered Ron's request that I remove my shoes for the occasion to show my disdain for formality. But I was forced to reject the concept, not wishing, no matter what others might think, to get my socks wet."

"What more can you do, Dick?"

"Well, Pat, the staff feels that I should be the subject of warm, earthy anecdotes of the kind the press told about Lyndon Johnson, but they haven't thought of any yet."

"Give them another month, Dick. Wait, what about that time you spilled catsup on your vest and said, "Darn it!"

"That type of language, in my judgment, is not necessary. But perhaps if I told a joke. Hmmm. Aha, listen! I have both won and lost. Winning is more fun.' What is your candid opinion of that joke, Pat?"

"I think it's the funniest joke you ever told, Dick."

"Thank you, Pat, for your confidence. I shall now, having slept my seven hours and thirty-two minutes as always, leap from my bed and devote my usual four minutes and forty-seven seconds to my breakfast so that I may stride to work. Please order my regular bowl of cottage cheese and catsup."

"Wait, Dick. I have a good idea. Why not have breakfast in bed this morning?"

"What is breakfast in bed, Pat?"

"Many people have breakfast in bed, Dick. It will give you a warmly human image that will capture the hearts of all Americans. I'll call the photographers."

"By golly, Pat, you are right. Wait till I adjust this pillow behind me. There. Now, how can any fair-minded person say that I am not a regular fellow, one of the guys. How do I look?"

"Fine, Dick. But maybe if you just loosened your necktie . . ."

It was my contention that while Nixon wanted desperately to be accepted, he was not about to shed the hard-wrought shell of dignity that the necktie symbolized—a shell that prevented others from getting too close. His necktie went with his pontifical manner of speaking, and his fear of rejection was reflected in his attempts to placate all factions capable of being placated. This drive to ingratiate himself gave him at times a certain Uriah Heep quality that opened him to good, vicious satire. Here's an example based on his statement at the Arkansas-Texas "game of the century" in 1969 that there was nothing he would like better than to be a football broadcaster:

"Well, I see that down on the field time is back in, it seems to me. I would say that Texas has the ball . . . I don't want to prejudge the officials on this. I don't always agree with the officials. Many decent Americans don't. But let me point out that what the officials say is, in my opinion, the law, and it is the duty of a sportscaster, in my judgment, to uphold the law, whether he agrees with it or not.

"But I would say that Texas has the ball in the vicinity of, as I indicated in an earlier statement to you at that time, the Arkansas forty-two yard line. I say this somewhat cautiously as I do not want to preclude the hopes of the millions of Arkansas fans, whom Pat and I admire highly, that Arkansas may, at some point in the future, also have the ball. But at this time, that would be my observation.

"Yes, Texas, I'm proud to say, does have the ball. The quarterback is fading back to—and I do not say this to limit his options in any way—pass. Yes, he has instituted a pass and, quite candidly, it is the finest pass I have ever seen. A perfect spiral, it seems to me.

"By this, I do not mean to detract in any manner from the Arkansas quarterback, who has also thrown many of the finest passes I have ever, in my judgment, seen. All perfect spirals, it seems to me.

"Well, there's the final gun, my fellow Americans. The two number one teams in the country are now staging a planned withdrawal from the field just as I confidently predicted they would do at this time.

"Let me be perfectly honest on one thing: I do not think this is the time or the place, in my judgment, to make any emotional statement as to who won or who lost this game of the century here today.

"In my opinion, this would amount to kicking the loser when he was down. I have never kicked losers when they are down, and I do not intend to institute such a policy here today. That is my position on this, rightly or wrongly."

And so on. But no one ever questioned the doggedness of Nixon's determination. To me, his drive seemed not so much for power—that Holy Grail for most politicians—but to prove officially through the ballot box that the majority of the people liked, respected and accepted him. That's why his defeats were so painful. That's why his victory in 1968 was so satisfying. Only six short years before, he had been written off as the defeated candidate for governor of California, doomed to become a wealthy Wall Street lawyer. I'm sure that this was what Pat Nixon would have preferred. I watched her for all those years seated on all those podiums at all those campaign stops. The thin blonde hair, the pale skin you felt you could see through … She struck me as very fragile, very wispy and very unhappy. She would gaze up at her husband at the rostrum with the same adoring look year after year. She would clap at the right time and smile at the same joke no matter how many times he repeated it, but her mind always seemed far away. She was a gracious woman and performed her chores as first lady dutifully and well, but I always felt sorry for her. What her relationship with her husband was, I can only guess. In public, it was a one-armed relationship. In moments of victory, he would put one arm over her shoulders and wave the other at the crowd, but I can't recall ever seeing him with both arms around her. Author and editor Michael Korda tells of having lunch in the Nixons' apartment in the early '80s. He, Mrs. Nixon and Julie Nixon Eisenhower were seated at the table when Nixon entered. He greeted his wife, wrote Korda, by shaking her hand and saying, "Nice to see you." I was always surprised that the Nixons had children.

If his wife was adverse to politics, it didn't affect Nixon. By the mid-'60s he was doggedly traveling all over the country, delivering addresses for local candidates and otherwise building credits to run again for president. I figured he had a speech problem—he couldn't leave the stuff alone. In a series called "The Comeback Kid," he would wander down to the corner to talk to the boys, but one word would lead to another, and before Pat knew it, he would be off on a coast-to-coast speaking binge. Finally, he hit bottom and threw his hat in the ring for the presidency. Pat, of course, was appalled. "Oh, please dear," she pleads, "renounce temptation forever and stay at home in the bosom of your loving family."

"I cannot," says Dick, striking a noble pose, "for there is a Higher Law, which no man can deny, that says this time, I shall win."

"What law is that?" asks poor Pat.

"The law," says Dick, "of averages."

Once he had squeaked by Hubert Humphrey and taken his seat in the Oval Office, it would seem as though he had at last been accepted by his fellow citizens. That drive in him should finally be stilled. There was no question that he relished all the perks of office. One of the first acts of this poor Whittier boy who had risen to become president was to order Graustarkian uniforms designed for the White House police—uniforms that suggested the Swiss Guard who protected the Pope. Here was a nerd's idea of prestigious splendor, and it was quickly shot down by the hateful press.

On his inauguration day, the wonderful cartoonist Herblock gave the new president a shave, and I, like a good many of my betters, wrote a column saying that victory may well have engendered a genuinely new Nixon whose intelligence and drive would lead the nation to untrammeled heights. Up there on the rostrum, he seemed to glow. Then I watched his limousine roll ponderously down Pennsylvania Avenue in the inaugural parade. In my memory, it is dark and low, and the thick, rolled-up bullet-proof windows have a greenish tinge, like the bottoms of bottles. Cocooned deep within was our new president, our hope for the future.

In private, Nixon was still a far different man. What appalled me about the Watergate tapes was not so much what Nixon said, but the way he said it. Here was the man who had excoriated Harry Truman in 1960 for saying "hell" in public. Nixon said at the time that when he was in the White House, people would say, "Well there's a man who maintains the kind of standards personally that I would want my child to follow." But on listening to the tapes, you could picture Nixon, his feet up on his desk, growling at Ehrlichman and Haldeman in locker-room language. Yet he seemed to spout the obscenities awkwardly, as though he were making a conscious effort to sound like one of the boys.

Much of what we are is reflected in the way we see others. Nixon saw his fellow humans as a gaggle of connivers. In politics, of course, he was often right—conniving being in the nature of the game. With this outlook, his penchant for secrecy was not surprising. A good example was his secret bombing of Cambodia in 1969. The bombing was no secret to the pilots who dropped the bombs or to the Cambodian peasants on which they fell. Neither was it a secret to Hanoi, Phnom Penh or Moscow. It was only a secret to the American people and the Congress. I think Nixon enjoyed that. His conviction that manipulating the public through secrecy and distortions was ethically permissible was reflected in his numerous books of autobiography. In *Six Crises*, he tells how he became "mad at Kennedy—personally" during the 1960 campaign. What angered him, Nixon said, was that Kennedy stole his idea of invading Cuba. As Nixon told it, when the CIA briefed Kennedy on the secret plan, Kennedy promptly began extolling it on campaign platforms as his plan. "What could I do?" asks Nixon in the book. "One course," he wrote, would be to tell the voters precisely what his policy toward Cuba would be. "But this," he said, "would be, for me, an utterly irresponsible act." Another course might be to keep quiet about the secret plans and simply say that a number of alternatives for dealing with Cuba was under consideration. That course is not mentioned in the book.

"There was only one thing I could do," Nixon wrote. "The covert operation must be protected at all costs.... I must attack Kennedy on his proposal."

Say what you will about Mr. Nixon, when he attacks a proposal, he attacks it all out, even if it's his own. Checking my notes, I found that on October 21, 1960, in New York, he attacked the proposal as "probably the most dangerously irresponsible one that he [Kennedy] has made." The next day in Pennsylvania, Nixon called the proposal "a direct invitation for the Soviet Union to intervene militarily on the side of Castro." To cap it off, he then challenged Kennedy to a fifth television debate exclusively on this "matter of great public interest—Cuba." It was clear that Nixon felt he had a winner in excoriating the policy he planned to carry out when he became president.

That Nixon should take pride in having hoodwinked the public is a commentary on his view of political candor. At the time the book came out, Kennedy called it "hogwash" and stoutly claimed that the invasion of Cuba was his idea. Why the two men fought over credit for a policy that resulted in the Bay of Pigs is one of those minor mysteries of politics.

"If only someone had loved him," Henry Kissinger said of Nixon, "he might have become a truly great man." As it was, *Time* magazine saluted him on his death as "the most important figure of the post-World War II era." It is perhaps a comment on our times that *Time* could so extol a man who was both a nerd and dork. Nixon undoubtedly would have loved *Time*'s eulogy. I'm not sure, though, that he wouldn't prefer to have been known as just one of the guys.

Chapter Twelve

Our Leaders, Long May They Rave

One effect of Watergate was to diminish interest in politics. In the decades that followed, a betrayed public participated less and less in the electoral process. I confess that my once-burning concern for the commonweal was at best a glowing ember. For one thing, it was hard to get worked up about Gerald Ford one way or another. Where Barry Goldwater had all the attributes of Superman, President Ford was another character entirely:

Is it a bird? Is it an aeroplane? No, it's Scoutmaster!
  Faster than a patent remedy, stronger than a square knot, able to leap over crass partisanship with a single homily, it's . . . Scoutmaster!
  As we join Scoutmaster today, he's seated in his new Oval Office disguised as a nice, stuffy, mild-mannered president. His secretary, Lotus Lane, who doesn't know his true identity, enters.
Lotus: Golly, Chief, the old president has left the country in a terrible mess. Inflation's running rampant. The elderly, the poor, the minorities are suffering. The young are hooked on drugs and sex. You simply have to do something!
Scoutmaster: (*frowning*) Gosh, (excuse my language, Lotus) you're right. But let me ask a technical question: What is sex?
Lotus: Oh, Chief, you're a nice guy, but you're hopeless. How I wish Scoutmaster were here.
Scoutmaster: (*after Lotus storms out*) Lotus is right! This sounds like a job for . . . Scoutmaster!

(*He steps into the phone booth next to his desk and whips off his stuffy old gray suit to reveal khaki shorts, merit badges and a forage cap, the uniform of Scoutmaster—the brains behind that super-secret organization, The Good Scouts of America.*

(*Leaping into his trusty Model A, he rushes to Capitol Hill. Oh, how the congressmen cheer this symbol of the country's salvation!*)

SCOUTMASTER: (*sternly*) Time for a little straight talk, gang. In this hour of crisis, we've all got to be Good Scouts.

To restore faith in government, we must be trustworthy and loyal. We must think of the problems of the elderly and be helpful when they want to cross the street. And when it comes to the colored, no matter what color they may be, let us resolve to be courteous, kind, obedient and cheerful at all times.

As for inflation, it can be solved only if we uphold the Good Scout Law and be thrifty. And, while we're at it, gang, let's all be clean, brave, clean and reverent, too, because those are nice things to be.

As for me, on my honor, I will do my best to do my duty to God and my country and to obey The Good Scout Law.

(*Pandemonium reigns as Democrats and Republicans embrace tearfully while Scoutmaster slips back to his Oval Office and resumes his disguise.*)

LOTUS: (*entering with a newspaper*) Chief! Have you seen this? As a result of Scoutmaster's speech, General Motors has cut car prices 42 percent! George Meany has demanded a pay cut for all workers! The old president has donated his tape collection to the Smithsonian! Every hippie has shaved his beard! Teenagers have taken vows of premarital celibacy! And ghetto dwellers across the country are singing "We Are Overcome!"

SCOUTMASTER: Gee whiz, (excuse my language, Lotus), what is chastity?

LOTUS: Oh, Chief, you're so naive! Why can't you be stern like Scoutmaster?

SCOUTMASTER: (*winking into the camera*) Well, Lotus, we can't all be like Scoutmaster. (*turning serious*) But there's no reason we can't solve our problems overnight by all becoming Good Scouts—

trustworthy, loyal, helpful, friendly, courteous, kind,
obedient, cheerful, thrifty, clean, brave, clean and reverent.
LOTUS: You've got clean in there twice.
SCOUTMASTER: Darn, I never could get that straight.

On the one occasion I met President Ford, he proved to be a most likable man. It was at a cocktail party in Palm Springs, where he has lived in retirement since his White House years. It's perhaps not irrelevant that Palm Springs boasts more golf courses than schools and libraries combined. During the evening, he displayed a self-deprecatory humor, which every politician needs, even though he doesn't believe a single self-deprecatory word he utters. He often played golf with Bob Hope, and he regaled us with Hope's jokes about his game. ("Hope says I'm such a bad golfer that before I teed off the last time we played, I lost two balls in the ball washer.")

I had also been a fan of his wife, Betty, ever since I read an interview with her in *People* magazine in which she happily confided that Ford had taken their older kids to a baseball game while she was giving birth to their youngest child. "Do you now think you should have demanded that he stay home," the interviewer asked.

"Oh, no," replied my second favorite wife in the whole world, "because I don't believe that when you marry a person you should attempt to change his personality."

She went on to say she really loved the big galoot and was always glad to see him when he got a chance to drop by their home in Palm Springs. "But there are times," she admitted, "if he's here, say, fourteen days in a row, I begin to wonder whether he ought to be on the road so I can get a little more done."

Now there was a marriage made in heaven or some other place I'm not familiar with. In 1979, I turned out a column that began with the ex-president bouncing down to breakfast:

"What a beautiful morning," he says, "and what are your
plans for the day?"

"Well, dear," says Betty, blushing modestly, "I
thought I just might have a baby."

"Wonderful! Wonderful!" he says, rubbing his hands.

"I've always said every girl should have a hobby."

"I'm glad you're pleased, dear," she says, "and after breakfast, what would you like to do?"

"Me? Oh, it's such a nice day I thought I'd take in a baseball game. Say! Would you like to come?"

"No, I think I'm going to have a baby."

"Oh, that's right. Well, you go right ahead and do what you want. Don't you worry about me. I guess I can find my way out to the ballpark all right."

"Golly, you're so unselfish, Jerry. I don't suppose … I don't know quite how to say this. But I don't suppose you'd like to be nearby while I have my baby, would you?"

"Good gosh, Betty, what for? I know as much about having babies as you know about baseball."

"Of course, dear. It was just a silly thought. After all, it'll do you good to get out. You've been cooped up with me for eight hours now. You run along. Have a nice day."

"Thank you, Betty. Have a nice baby."

To be sure, perhaps it didn't happen that way at all. What do I know? All I know is that for every happily married politician there's a saint.

Ah, how we humor writers rubbed our hands in eager anticipation when Jimmy Carter defeated dull old lovable Jerry Ford. Never had America had a born-again, Spanish-speaking, down-home nuclear physicist who was a peanut-farming agribusinessman as president, particularly not one named "Jimmy."

And that was but the hors d'oeuvre. His wife, Rosalynn, smiled as though she had a permanent Excedrin headache. His no-nonsense mother, Miz Lillian, was fresh out of the Peace Corps. His daughter, Amy, had a dog named Grits to show she loved the simple life. She also had a suite in the White House. Just down the hall were the two brothers and their wives. Jeff was living on an allowance. He was 24. Chip, 26, however, was employed. He made $3,000 a year working for the Democratic National Committee. A member of Mr. Carter's staff said Jeff and Chip were the first two president's children ever to live in the White House who were married. They were also the first two president's children ever to live in the White House who qualified for food stamps.

Rounding out this delightful family were (1) Jimmy's Uncle Buddy, who, at 88, was promoting a film called *Peanuts*, in which he would star with his peanut-eating dog; (2) Jimmy's sister Ruth, a faith healer; (3) Jimmy's sister Gloria, a simple, ordinary housewife who rode a motorcycle and had a son in jail; and, of course, (4) Jimmy's funny, lovable, beer-drinking brother Billy, who said he didn't give a fig for fame and fortune just before he signed a contract with the Top Billing Company, a Nashville talent agency.

Here, surely, was a collection of targets to rival the Beverly Hillbillies. Joy abounded in the tiny hearts of satirists from coast to coast. I immediately launched a new series of columns entitled "Just Plains Folks," in honor of the president's home town in Georgia.

As topics of humor, however, the entire Carter family turned out in no time at all to be duller than deregulation of natural gas. On looking through the files, I see I did only half a dozen columns on "Just Plains Folks" before tossing in the sponge. To this day, I'm not sure what blighted the glowing prospects. For one thing, all the relatives but Billy disappeared from public view. I could only assume that presidential aides had locked them up in some pleasant room where they idled away the hours watching *Queen for a Day* and playing fish. As for Billy, it soon became apparent he had psychological problems that exempted him from being a figure of fun. As for the president himself, it wasn't that no one in American really liked him; the trouble was that no one in America really disliked him. And so it was that a miasma settled over the nation's humor writers.

Thank God for Ronald Reagan. Here's a column that captured the nation's mood, and mine, the day after his election:

> I woke up Wednesday morning to the sounds of my dear wife, Glynda, cheerily singing "America, the Beautiful" down in the kitchen. The sun was shining, the birds were singing, and, sure enough, when I reached the breakfast nook, beaming up at me from my plate were two perfect double-yolked eggs.

"Gosh, Glynda," I couldn't help saying, "it's sure great being an American again."

"Yes, dear," she agreed, expertly rolling out dough for a scrumptious apple pie, "I love being feared and respected all over the world."

"And strong at home, too," I reminded her. "Gee, I feel as sound as a dollar."

"Speaking of dollars, dear," she said, wiping her hands on her starched white apron, "would you mind if I gave up my job as chief of neurosurgery at the university? I just want to devote full time to taking care of you and our two wonderful children, Mordred and Malphasia."

"Heck, no, darling," I said. "I believe it's the job of us men to keep you girls happy. And don't you worry your pretty little head about the money. Our 30 percent tax cut will more than take care of that—especially now that we don't have to be scared of inflation or unemployment or Malphasia not getting straight A's."

Well, speak of the cute little devil! Malphasia bounced into the room, wearing new saddle shoes, a pleated skirt, a cashmere cardigan and cultured pearls. "Hi, Mom; hi, Daddykins," she said. "Is it OK if I have my Moral Betterment gang over tonight for Bosco and Oreos? We're making up Thanksgiving baskets for the poor colored people."

"That's nice, dear," said Glynda, "but I think they prefer being called Negroes. You must ask your father, though. He knows best."

"To tell the truth," I said frowning, "I was hoping we could all have dinner out together at McDonald's and take in a movie. *Gidget Goes to Washington* is at the Roxie and it's Dish Nite."

"I've seen it three times, Dad," said Mordred, coming in from the garage and rubbing his manly hand through his crew-cut hair. "But I'd love to see it again if you want. Excuse me for being late for breakfast, Mom, but I was washing the car."

"No, Mordred," I said, trying not to sound disappointed. "If you've seen it, and Malphasia would rather have her little friends over ..."

But that Malphasia, gosh darn her! She could tell I was a teensy bit hurt. Suddenly she brightened. "I know," she cried, "we can put on our own show! I'll get out my Lawrence Welk records and ..."

"Right!" chimed in Mordred. "Mom can teach us the Lambeth Walk, and Dad can tell us again how he used to stack groceries for 60 cents an hour. I love that story."

"Well," I said to Glynda when breakfast was over, "I guess it's time to mosey down to the office and type up a little column about the results of the presidential election."

"Have a nice day, dear," said Glynda. "And don't work too hard."

"I won't," I promised with a happy smile, "for the next four years."

I was also delighted when Mr. Reagan, who posed as a devoted family man, finally had his first glimpse of his new granddaughter. She was twenty-one months old at the time. And why hadn't he laid eyes on her until she was approaching her second birthday? The president addressed his keen, analytical mind to the question. "Our problem was mainly one of distance," he said, "and so when we eliminated the distance, we eliminated the problem."

My dear wife, Glynda, I said in a column, was equally delighted. She dearly loves our grandchildren, as long as their parents remain in the room, but she figures she's paid her dues, and she will go to any lengths to avoid baby-sitting with them. I was therefore surprised when she said the president was absolutely right, and he had inspired her to call our son, Mordred, to tell him to bring his daughter, Pandora, over.

"Not tonight," I said, "I've got a headache."

"No," said Glynda. "I mean once every twenty-one months."

With his inauguration, my first task was to devise a series of scenarios that captured his presidency. I was tempted to revive Sir

Ronald of Holyrude, that innocent who had never seen a budget, but Mr. Reagan, as the leader of the free world, seemed a cut above such naiveté. True, although he had been governing and touring the hustings for close to two decades, he was still campaigning as the honest citizen against the evil professional politicians, so I tried to capture that in a dozen movies, all called "Mr. Reagan Goes to Washington."

Those who saw the first rushes, I wrote, were ecstatic. "Fears that Ronald Reagan was too old to play Ronald Reagan have now been dispelled," said the New York Times. "He is still perfection in the role he has played for more than half a century, that of the lovable, all-American nice guy."

"Nancy Davis socko in Mrs. R.R. part," said Variety. "Forget Wyman."

The Jimmy Stewart role fit Mr. Reagan to a T, and Mrs. Reagan was perfect as the Beautiful Girl Who Loves Him. Minor characters included Teddy Kennedy as the Spoiled Rich Kid who sneers at Ronnie behind his back and is secretly out to get him, and Ronnie's endearing sidekick and "go-fer," George Bush, who keeps whining, "Well, what will we do now, Ronnie?"

In one of the very first scenes, Producer Cecil B. DeMeese asks Ronnie if a black should be given a major role. "Sure," says Ronnie. "A black what?" But Ronnie does hire a black to serve in the White House. He will serve breakfast, lunch and dinner.

Mr. Reagan was such a seasoned actor I saw no reason he couldn't star in not one but two series. So in addition to "Mr. Reagan Goes to Washington," I began running a soap opera entitled "The Golden Years." It asked the question "Can an aging, unemployed B-movie actor find happiness running the free world?" The answer was invariably yes. During the 1980 campaign, when the subject of Mr. Reagan's age came up, he had promised that, if elected, he would be tested periodically for senility and would "step down" if he had "any feeling at all that (his) capabilities had been reduced." Many of the plots of "The Golden Years" were built on that pledge by Mr. Reagan, for I thought that promising to remember to be tested for senility was a delightful gambit. Here's how they went:

RONNIE: Good morning ... uh ... uh ...

NANCY: I'm "Nancy," dear.

RONNIE: Yes, of course, Nancy Dear. Let's see, what was I looking for?

NANCY: Your breakfast, dear. And here it is, piping hot.

RONNIE: (*cheerfully buttering his tie*) My favorite! Bacon and whatchamacallems.

NANCY: I hate to bring this up, but isn't there something you've been forgetting?

RONNIE: (*frowning*) I don't think so. Let me check. Jacket, shirt, shoes, socks, trousers ... Darn! I'll slip into a pair right now. (*opening a door*) Hey! What are all these pots and pans doing in my closet?

NANCY: Your trousers are upstairs, dear. But I was speaking of your forgetting one of your campaign promises.

RONNIE: (*indignantly*) I never forget a campaign promise! That's because I keep a list of them with me at all times. (*frowning*) Now where did I put that list?

NANCY: It's in your hand, dear.

RONNIE: It's in my hand, dear. Hmmm. "Ct. Txs.," "Inc. Dfnse. Spndng" and ... What do you think "Bal. Bdgt." means?

NANCY: I think you promised to balance the budget, and you have come within a trillion or so. But isn't there something on your list about a "Sen. Test."?

RONNIE: Where? Oh, on my list. I'll take a look. "Inc. Bus. Invest," "Create Prosp." What gibberish. Here's a funny one: "Sen. Test." Did I promise to test a senator?

NANCY: No, dear. You promised ... I hesitate to say this, but you promised to take periodic tests to make sure you weren't forgetting things.

RONNIE: Gosh, that was a great promise. How did my tests turn out?

NANCY: I'm afraid you forgot to take any.

RONNIE: Well, that's easily remedied. I'll go take one right now. (*opening door*) What are all these sheets doing on the front steps, Nellie Dear?

NANCY: It's "Nancy," dear. And I'm so happy that at last you're
going to take that test.
RONNIE: (*enfolding her in his arms*) It makes me happy to make
you happy, Nancy Dear. What test?

I was, of course, not the only one to question Mr. Reagan's
intellectual capacity. Not long after his inauguration, the British
began running a weekly television series entitled *The President's
Brain Is Missing*. As a patriotic American, I naturally took offense.
The president's brain was not missing, I coldly informed our British
cousins; it had merely been misplaced.

"On numerous occasions," I quoted a White House source as
saying, "the president has been able to find his glasses, his keys and
his hearing aid, which he often wears into the shower. We are quite
confident that his brain will turn up sooner or later."

Besides, I said, Mr. Reagan had a lopsided grin, a boyish toss of
the head and Mrs. Reagan to tell him what to say. The last thing he
needed was a brain. Does Queen Elizabeth have a brain? Who
knows? Who cares? The last British monarch to have a brain brought
the entire Spanish Armada down on that tiny island. And there
hasn't been a brain in the House of Lords since Pitt the Elder. Where
do leaders with brains get you? They get you to places like Waterloo
and Watergate. Peter the Great, who had one of the biggest brains in
modern history, managed to get twelve million people killed before
he shuffled off to his reward. Who needs brains?

We Americans got along just fine, thank you, with presidents
who didn't get all worked up about brains. Our most prosperous
and peaceful times in this century were under Calvin Coolidge,
Dwight Eisenhower and Ronald Reagan. *Res ipsa loquitor*. If we
wanted a president with brains, by golly, we'd elect one.

As luck would have it, the president's brain soon turned up. It
was discovered in his jelly bean jar by young Eddie Hockness, a very
junior White House aide whose job it was to remove the green jelly
beans as Mr. Reagan never cared for green jelly beans.

"I spotted it right away," said young Eddie. "It was much too big to
be in there. In fact, it was twice the size of an ordinary old jelly bean."

Unfortunately, Eddie didn't bother to notify the White House staff of his discovery. ("I didn't think it was worth mentioning," he later said a bit sullenly.) Consequently, Reagan's aides didn't realize the president had his brain back until that fateful radio program in August of 1984. As usual, he had been carefully fed a prepared address, but when asked for a voice level, he responded, "My fellow Americans, I am pleased to tell you that I just signed legislation which outlaws Russia forever. The bombing begins in five minutes."

At the time, I thought this just another funny presidential quip that might or might not start World War III. Far more prescient was top aide Michael Deaver. "My God," a pale Deaver told Chief of Staff James Baker, "the president's found his brain!"

Plans were laid to sneak up on the president when he was asleep—perhaps at the next cabinet meeting—kidnap his brain and hide it somewhere around the White House where it would never be found, such as among the State Department's foreign policy briefing papers. The fear, of course, was that the president would become so elated at having a brain that he might actually attempt to use it. Fortunately, for the good of the nation, that never happened.

But you couldn't convince the Democrats. During the Iran-Contra hearings, they stooped to a new low in political vitriol: They flatly accused the president of the United States of knowing what was going on. Naturally, Mr. Reagan and his staff vociferously denied it. Sure, Admiral Poindexter had briefed the president every morning on national security matters, but not once did he see fit to mention that we were swapping arms for hostages with Iran or using secret funds to illegally supply the Contras in Nicaragua. Why bother Mr. Reagan's new-found brain with petty details?

Needless to say, the Democrats were not about to accept such a defense. As the hearings dragged on and Mr. Reagan continued insisting he couldn't remember ever knowing what was going on, my friend Mary Reilly summed up the tenor of the entire scandal in a single question: "What did the president forget," she asked, "and when did he forget it?"

That was such a fascinating question that, in 1987, I envisioned a sequel to that long-ago classic movie, *Fantastic Voyage*, in which three brave scientists—Stephen Boyd, William Redfield and Raquel

Welch—are miniaturized to the size of microbes to penetrate a human body. In the sequel, it is White House Chief of Staff Don Regan who injects them into Mr. Reagan's left ear. Their goal: to penetrate the labyrinth of the president's brain, seek out his memory bank and determine what's missing.

Once inside, the three bold adventurers chop their way through the tough meninges, cut across the gray wastes of the cortex to find themselves in the vast (to them) cerebrum. "It's quiet—too quiet," mutters Miss Welch nervously, her voice echoing in the dark emptiness.

"Drop flat!" shouts the muscular Dr. Boyd as the brain tissue around them convulses in a giant shudder that threatens to crush them all. "It's a passing thought!"

"My God!" sobs Miss Welch. "I can't take another one of those."

"It's OK, Raquel," says Dr. Redfield, embracing her. "We've got seven minutes until the next one."

The trio struggles on up a narrow, treacherous neural path, scaling the precipitous face of a towering humility and skirting a bottomless well of winsome boyishness. At last they come upon what looks like a large, old-fashioned computer, its big vacuum tubes faintly glowing.

"It's the memory bank," cries Dr. Redfield triumphantly. "Let's see what we've got."

But after pushing scores of buttons, Dr. Boyd throws up his hands. "All that's in there is a Ronald Reagan Film Festival. Let's push on."

"Wait," says Miss Welch, tears in her eyes, "I want to see the last reel of *Hellcats of the Navy*."

An exasperated Dr. Boyd sets out ahead and— "Aiyee!"—disappears before their very eyes. The other two rush forward to find the scientist clinging desperately to a flimsy projection of gray matter below the lip of a yawning chasm.

"Good Lord, it's an eighteen-month memory gap!" says Dr. Redfield, peering into the depths. "And down there at the bottom is a sprawling jumble of the missing items we've been looking for."

After rescuing Dr. Boyd, the three explorers rappel down to the treasure below and begin taking inventory of what the president forgot in the past year-and-a-half.

"Location of Botswana," calls out Dr. Redfield as Miss Welch takes notes. "And here's an autographed Bible with Best Wishes to A.

"His granddaughter," says Dr. Boyd, ticking off items. "Why he came into the room and fourteen private cottage cheese lunches with Oliver North."

"And here's a meeting with a top aide," added Dr. Redfield. "That's when he remembered to forget about approving the Iran arms deal."

"Name of current White House pet," says Dr. Boyd, picking up one forgotten item after another. "Informing Congress about what was going on, who is current White House chief of staff and why . . . Quick, let's get out of here. Another passing thought is due to strike at any minute!"

Space precludes detailing their harrowing escape. At the end, they emerge from the president's right ear onto a slide held by Don Regan. Regan carefully lifts the slide to his own ear and listens as the tiny, tiny voice of Dr. Redfield itemizes the items the president forgot one by one.

When he finishes, Regan shakes his head sadly. "I fear the mission has failed," he says somberly.

"Nothing on the slide?" asks an aide.

Regan holds the slide to his lips and blows. "Not now," he says.

In fairness, President Reagan was loyally backed by his vice president, George Bush. Mr. Bush said he sure as heck didn't know what was going on either. Naturally, we elected Mr. Bush the next president of the United States.

After eight years of President Reagan, Mr. Bush was a distinct disappointment to us humor writers. Who needs a polite, well-meaning soul as a target? By scratching desperately, we were able to attack only his syntax, his clinging to Mr. Reagan's coattails, his striving to offend no one and his laughable attempts to depict himself as

a common man. As early as the 1988 campaign, I had devised the
scenario for a new series, "Lifestyle of the Rich and Humble." It
asked the question "Can a man born with a silver spoon in his
mouth eat pork rinds properly?" Here's the first one:

> *As we join George today, he is entering the breakfast room*
> *of the palatial vice presidential residence. His charming wife,*
> *Barbara, waits to greet him.*
>
> GEORGE: (*pounding his fist on the breakfast table*) I care not
> what others may say. I say it's a nice day!
>
> BARBARA: Good for you, dear. I love your new fiercely
> independent spirit now that you're running for president.
> How would you like your eggs?
>
> GEORGE: I don't give a fig what people may think. I'll have
> my eggs exactly the way I like them—which is exactly the
> way the president likes his, whatever way that may be.
>
> BARBARA: Scrambled, I think. Which reminds me, I see by
> the papers that you've decided to favor a veto of that civil
> rights legislation after thinking it over for only a month.
>
> GEORGE: Yes, it was a very complex issue, and it took the
> president a month to make up my mind.
>
> BARBARA: But isn't that a controversial position?
>
> GEORGE: (*thrusting forth his chin*) To H-e-double-toothpicks
> with fickle public opinion. No matter what the cost, it's my
> bounden duty to stand behind the most popular president
> since George Washington.
>
> BARBARA: That's a very courageous pose, dear. You look so ...
> so Reaganesque. I know you're going to win in November.
> Now all you have to do is appeal to the common people.
>
> GEORGE: (*hitching up his Mark Cross belt*) By gosh, that reminds
> me of a story. Well, now, I grew up in a little two-debutante
> town in Texas that was so poor the ratty old polo field was all
> chewed up and the washroom attendant down at the golf club
> handed out paper towels. So one day ... Where was I?
>
> BARBARA: That's a very Reaganesque anecdote, dear, particularly
> the ending. But didn't you grow up in a fancy New York suburb
> in Connecticut?

GEORGE: There, too. Well, I think I'll go out by the gazebo and get my exercise. Has the brush arrived yet?

BARBARA: I ordered another truckload yesterday, but it hasn't come yet. If you want to cut something, why don't you just mow the lawn?

GEORGE: (*with dignity*) The president and I don't do lawns. There must be something else, though. Golly, what an insoluble problem.

BARBARA: Well, you could demonstrate your new fiercely independent, decisive spirit by independently deciding what the president does when faced with an insoluble problem.

GEORGE: (*smacking his fist into his palm*) Great idea! But don't forget to wake me for lunch.

I confess that I made no attempt to capture Mr. Bush's syntax. Others had done the job only too well. I particularly liked White House correspondent Maureen Dowd's collection for the *New York Times*. Here's the president rhapsodizing about a tour of the Lincoln bedroom he had given Czech president Vaclav Havel: "And the look on his face, as the man who was in jail and dying, or living—whatever—for freedom, stood out there, hoping against hope for freedom."

That compared favorably to his pledge that he would "make sure that everyone who has a job wants a job," and his description of his relationship with President Reagan: "For seven-and-a-half years I have worked alongside him, and I am proud to be his partner. We have had triumphs, we have made mistakes, we have had sex." This latter perhaps ties in with his statement on being defeated for the Senate in 1970: "I am looking introvertedly, and I don't like what I see." But I think he better summed himself up in an interview in the *New York Times Magazine*: "I am not," he said, "your basic intellectual."

And he wasn't. He was a pleasant, likable man with no particular ideology or fervent convictions of his own. If he subscribed to any credo, it was "For God, for Country and for Yale," which Harvard alumnus Eliott Richardson once described as "the most anti-climactic statement of all time." As best he could, he did what was expected of him. He married well, became a navy combat pilot and went into politics because his father, a famous senator, expected it of him. He did as well or better than expected as congressman, ambassador and CIA director. As vice president, no one could have been expected to be more loyal and self-effacing. It was only as president that he came a cropper. He seemed another embodiment of the Peter Principle—that in a hierarchy each of us tends to rise to the level of our incompetence. For the first time in his life, he didn't do what was expected of him. So the public elected Bill Clinton.

From the start, I had problems with Mr. Clinton. My main problem was that I didn't like him. After twelve years of the rich getting richer and the poor getting poorer, most of his political program won my wholehearted support. If he didn't have all the answers, at least he was raising the right questions. But I didn't like him.

My first doubts were raised when he was asked if he had ever smoked marijuana. "I have never broken the laws of the United States," he replied nobly. Now, that's sort of an odd response, but it was accepted at the time and so the matter rested. It turned out later that he had smoked marijuana in England, although he didn't— God forbid—inhale. To me, his initial answer was unforgivably devious. His protestations that he didn't—God forbid—inhale the marijuana made him the first person I ever heard of who smoked pot for the flavor.

My feelings about him were reinforced by the haircut incident As you may recall, he hired a $200 Hollywood hairdresser to cut his hair aboard Air Force One while it sat on the tarmac in Los Angeles for an hour. Two aspects of this bothered me: First, while he held up no commercial flights as originally reported, he did force his staff, the press and the plane's crew to twiddle their thumbs for an hour while he had his hair cut. I thought this inconsiderate at best. Second, who needs a $200 haircut? For the past thirty years, I've had my hair cut by Joe Sanchez in his one-man shop off the *Chronicle* lobby. He's gone up from $3 to $9 but he's well worth it. A dozen years ago, a barber in the backwoods of China did an excellent job on me for the equivalent of six cents, and not once did he talk about the Giants' chances. Those who need $200 haircuts are Hollywood actors and others who think they are God's gift to women. Those who have $200 haircuts are those who have tawdry affairs with publicity-seeking bimbos and who might well invite one of them up to his hotel room, expecting her to eagerly perform fellatio. Nor do I care much for the image projected by his aggressive wife. A Republican friend described her as a cross between Eleanor Roosevelt and Eva Peron. Andrew Lloyd Webber, he said, was even then writing a new musical, *Hillary!* ("Don't cry for me, Arkansas ...")

Having salved my soul by ridding it of all this vituperation, I should add that I'm sure the Clintons in person are, like most politicians, professionally quite likable. Never having met them, however, I was, like a good portion of the public, able to enjoy disliking them with considerable relish.

Unfortunately, this affected the columns I wrote about them. I think it was Russell Baker who told me, "You have to love your villains." In satire, it certainly helps. I felt much more comfortable attacking Presidents Kennedy, Johnson and Reagan, all of whom I liked, than poor Mr. Nixon. The problem, of course, is that your assaults become too vicious, and you are in danger of bludgeoning your victim with blunt polemics rather than skewering him with the razor-sharp rapier you know you have somewhere in your arsenal. Presidents you don't like, I've found, are bad for your image.

And so it was with Mr. Clinton since the beginning. During the 1992 campaign, I contended he constantly displayed the smile of a sneering rabbit, particularly when talking about the atrocities in Bosnia. In an effort to capture the spirit of his electioneering with Al Gore, I began a series entitled "The Hearty Boys." Here's a sample:

> Bill Hearty stepped down from the RV. A little smile played across his handsome face as he ran his fingers through his curly blond hair.
>
> "Gosh, wasn't that a great trip, Al?" he enthused, smiling. "When I was a boy, we were too poor to afford an RV with indoor plumbing—or indoor plumbing either, for that matter."
>
> His brother, Al, was equally handsome in his dark, serious way. "Yes, Bill," he agreed, frowning, "but now it is time to hit the old campaign trail."
>
> "Sure, Al," acceded Bill, smiling. "But wasn't that a swell send-off party they gave us in New York? What

about that cute little gal who promised me a lay when we get to Hawaii?"

"That was a lei, Bill," corrected Al, frowning. "And I thought you swore off for the duration."

"That was junk food, Al," averred Bill, smiling. "As for girls ... Why, here they are now."

Emerging from the RV were pretty, blonde Hillary and pretty, blonde Tipper. "The really swell thing about this trip is that Hillary and I got to know each other," burbled Tipper. "I always thought she was just a stuffy old head library monitor."

"And I always thought Tipper was just a silly, air-head cheerleader," snapped Hillary.

"And you both changed your minds?" inquired Bill, smiling.

"What's for dinner?" snapped Hillary.

"Oh, go bake a cookie," burbled Tipper.

"Not so fast, girls," cautioned Al, frowning. "Bill and I have to throw a football around for the cameras first to show we are regular guys."

"When I was a boy, we were so poor we had to eat my football, and we all got scurvy and three of my cousins starved to death," rejoined Bill, smiling. He took out his gleaming saxophone. "Any requests?"

"Yes," snapped Hillary. "Could you for just ten god-damned minutes stop smiling?"

And so forth. If I alone disliked the Clintons, it would be of small matter, but my aversion was shared by an uncommon number of my friends, liberals and conservatives alike, including those in the national press. We crowed over his defeats and gave him little credit for his many accomplishments. I felt this, more than anything, affected his ability to govern. When Paula Jones accused him of gross misconduct in a hotel room, I confess that I was all too ready to believe her. It wasn't until I saw her being questioned on television that I began to have my doubts. It made me realize these scandals are cumulative. Because I disliked the man, I tended to believe each accusation, true or not, and, because I believed each accusation, my antipathy grew.

But enough of these ill feelings. Merely contemplating them makes me feel besmirched. Suffice it to say that they dulled the edge of satire. I struggled without success to invent a series that would capture the new president. I tried "As the World Jogs," "Billy Boomer, Boy President" and "Mr. Wonk Goes to Washington." Nothing seemed to work. The results were so dull that I can't bring myself to reprint a sample here.

What this country needs, I say, is a president who's a delight to attack. Dan Quayle has my vote. That's in keeping with the credo by which I cast my ballot for presidents: "Columnist First, American Second."

Chapter Thirteen

A KOSHER CAMELOT

When I was popping zits in high school, I was dead certain that nation states were an anachronism that would wither and blow away by the time I was middle-aged. World Federalism, that was the ticket. I confessed to a certain chauvinism where the United States was concerned. Its history was inspiring and its flag lovely, but I viewed it as only the best of an irrational lot. Why should the people living within an arbitrary set of invisible lines feel animosity toward people living in another arbitrary set of invisible lines? As the Egyptian astronaut noted years later, when viewed from outer space, the world has no national boundaries. So hooray for the UN. Huzzah for GATT, NAFTA and the EC. But what a small start we've made in abolishing the root cause of wars and cutthroat economic strife.

The only nation whose existence I was able to justify over the years was Israel. I was enamored by the stories of its citizen-soldiers with their homemade weapons licking the mighty Arab armies in 1948. Thanks to the film *Exodus*, I saw it as a nation of blonde, blue-eyed heroes who all looked like Paul Newman.[*] I was titillated by stories of new immigrants passing rocks to build walls. "Bitte, Herr Doctor," could be heard down the line. "Danke, Herr Doctor."

Then, in 1965, my budding love affair was consummated with a week-long trip to that Promised Land. I had drawn the plum of covering the opening of a new Hilton hotel in Tel Aviv, all expenses

---

[*] I will agree, though, that the movie was a bit long. Mort Sahl used to claim that when it entered its third hour, he tugged an usher's sleeve and whispered, "Let my people go!"

paid. Half a hundred news people and an equal number of celebrities from all over the place swooped in to take advantage of Mr. Hilton's generosity. One of the celebrities was a Mr. Radziwill. Legend had it that the Hilton staff had intended to invite the socially prominent Prince Radziwill, but that something had gone amiss and this was a distant cousin. While everything was on the house, we were asked to sign for food and drink so that the bookkeepers could shake down their equipment. Needless to say, we half a hundred newsmen signed "Radziwill" to every chit. While I've never seen the total, I'm confident that Mr. Radziwill can be credited with running up the most glorious bar bill in hotel history.

That was the week I met Chaim Topol, who went on to become the famous perennial star of *Fiddler on the Roof*. In 1965, he was a relatively unknown 30-year-old Israeli actor, but in that short week, he came to be one of the few men I've admired unreservedly. He summed up all that was best in the Israelis: He was funny and cynical, but with a burning idealism that for the most part he kept hidden as you would some precious jewel. His enthusiasm for people and ideas was boundless; he seemed to leap through life, never coming to rest for a moment. Yet he was devoted to his wife and children and to his Jewishness. He was plump even then, almost cherubic. He wore the Israeli national costume of sandals, khakis and a short-sleeved sport shirt, and he addressed everyone, from bellmen to parliamentarians, as "my dear friend." Moreover, he genuinely seemed to mean it. His humor was what I think of as "Israeli humor." It is to be distinguished from the traditional Jewish humor of Sholom Aleicheim, like that in *Fiddler on the Roof*. That humor is the sad, somewhat forlorn humor of a people who have been losing for two thousand years. Israeli humor is the humor of a people who are winning.

The first day I met Topol, he said he had just finished shooting a low-budget Israeli movie. I asked him what it was about. "Let's see," he said. "In the last scene we Israelis are bidding farewell to a wealthy American couple, Mr. and Mrs. Steinberg. They've come this vast distance to see the new Steinberg Memorial Forest, which their generosity has provided. We emotionally embrace them, praise them for making the desert green and promise that their munificent philanthropy will never be forgotten. After we have waved them off down the road, we put up a new sign. It says, 'Goldstein Memorial Forest,' and—hah!—up the road here come the Goldsteins!"

I thought this hilarious, and perhaps because he had found such an appreciative audience, Topol spent the week showing me around Israel in his battered car. It was a rich week. Two vignettes stand out: We were driving through Tel Aviv at night. A drunken man—a rare sight in Israel—staggered off the curb in the car's path. Topol slammed on the brakes and jumped out. For a moment, I thought I was about to see a fight, but Topol put his arm around the inebriate's shoulders. "You poor man," he said with genuine compassion. "You've had too much wine. You could have been killed." With that, he half-led him, half-carried him to the sidewalk and set him at rest on a flight of steps. "You should stay here until you feel better," he said.

When he got back in the car, I congratulated him on his humanitarian tolerance, but he shook his head. "I should have taken him home," he said.

The next day, we were driving through the countryside on our way to Jerusalem. The conversation turned to religion. Like 70 percent of the citizens of that religious state, Topol was not a religious man. Then what held Israel together? "You must know," he said, frowning, "that we are not a religion; we are a brotherhood." He pointed to a passing farm. "See those houses there? I can knock on any door in Israel, and they will share with me what they have. After two thousand years we at last have something of our own. We are no longer the outsiders. That's why I would gladly die . . ."

He caught himself, a bit embarrassed by this burst of emotionalism. Suddenly, he pointed to a figure on the side of the road. It was one of the Hasidim in his black hat, long black coat, beard and curling sideburns.

"Look! Look!" cried Topol.

"What?" I asked.

Topol's eyes were wide in mock horror. "A Jew!" he said.

Like all Israelis, Topol was inordinately proud of this supposed land of milk and honey. The northern half, I found, was mostly rocks and scraggle, but the southern half—ah, the southern half!—was an absolute desert. On the positive side was the climate. It was positively roasting in the summer and positively frigid in the winter. It was also dusty, noisy, poor and a political bedlam. It was bounded on one side by the sea and on the other by 50 million Arabs determined to slice every Israeli throat. At the time, I wrote a brief list of suggested answers to questions Israelis inevitably ask of foreign visitors:

Q: Weren't you surprised to see what a modern, prosperous, lush, verdant, wonderful country Israel is?

A: The view from Mt. Hermon is absolutely magnificent.

Q: Are you enjoying our lovely sunny climate?

A: To think that twenty years ago all this used to be desert.

Q: Here is another public housing project for immigrants. Aren't they beautiful buildings?

A: To think that twenty years ago all this used to be desert.

Q: See how many motor cars we now have on our roads?

A: What is the make of that truck coming at us? Head-on?

Yet even the Israelis could make light of the one thing their beloved little nation clearly lacked. It was from Topol that I first heard the joke that has become commonplace over the years: "If we were really the chosen people," he said with a grin, "instead of milk and honey, why couldn't the Good Lord have chosen to give us oil?"

Topol was fascinated with the column-writing business and did his best to think up topics for me. He felt Abe Nathan would make a fine subject. Nathan was a handsome former pilot who billed himself as the Hamburger King of Israel. Having introduced hamburgers to the previously hamburgerless nation at his California Cafe, Nathan was running for parliament on a daring peace plan. If elected, he pledged, he would fly his private biplane to Egypt, crash-land in Nasser's backyard and negotiate a peace treaty. After interviewing Nathan, I asked Topol if the Hamburger King could win.

"Oh," said Topol, "his noble proposal has won him fervent support."

"From whom?" I asked suspiciously.

"From," said Topol, "every other restaurant owner on the block."

Topol also introduced me to Ephraim Kishon, the Israeli satirist who wrote a column for *Ma'ariv*. Kishon, a slender, quiet young man, immediately became another of my heroes when I asked him if, like me, he wrote a daily column. "I write a daily column," said Kishon in words I've always dreamed of living by, "whenever I feel like it."

The week passed, as travel writers say, all too quickly. On the last day in Israel, I realized I hadn't written a word about the all-new Hilton hotel, to which I had sold my immortal soul. What was funny about this concrete and glass edifice, I asked myself in desperation. The answer in desperation came to me: It was kosher. Not only did it have two dining rooms—one for meat dishes and one for dairy foods—but it had a temperamental Swiss chef, M. Rene, who was dedicated to the hautest *haute cuisine*. The thick cookbook he would follow was the *kashrut*—the Jewish dietary laws. He would be assisted by two gentlemen known as the *Mashgichim*, who would observe his every move to make sure he never stirred a meat dish with a spoon that had ever touched a dairy product. Moreover, of course, the meat would have to soaked for three days in rock salt and water to make sure that every last drop of blood was drained from its fibers. I thought it would be amusing to see a temperamental chef struggling to create *tournedos avec buerre blanc* sans the *buerre blanc*. Unfortunately M. Rene was too temperamental to be interviewed, and who could blame him? So I talked to his superior, the hotel's director of food and beverages, for help in putting together a column on bloodless meat and butterless sauces in order to repay the Hilton people for my posh trip. "Please," said the food director in closing, "just say it doesn't *taste* kosher." Suffice it to say that I've never been invited to another Hilton hotel opening.

After a week of free liquor and a good deal of free time, my male colleagues were looking a bit the worse for wear when we boarded our homeward flight. The talk around the bar on the last night had been about "nice, damn it, Jewish girls.* Indeed, I'd advanced the theory that one of Israeli's gravest problems was nice Jewish girls. Here was a nation of two million souls surrounded by 50 million angry Arabs who were breeding like mad. And so on. But the view of

------

* A girl in those long-ago sexist days was any female under forty, and what a lovely word it was. Today, we politically correct authors are reduced to writing phrases like "our American boys and women in our fighting forces." There are times when I consider becoming a militant masculinist.

my combat-weary colleagues was better summed up by my seatmate, a determined young reporter, who looked out the window as
our plane lifted from the tarmac and said with a wave of his hand
and a sigh: "Farewell, land of the immaculate conception."

My love affair with that scraggly slice of real estate continued
to blossom as the years passed. I was thrilled by the astounding
Israeli successes during the Six-Day War in 1967. I thought my
Jewish friends at home stood straighter. No longer was the stereotypical Jew a shuffling, bearded European outcast. Now he was a
brave, handsome young soldier standing straddle-legged atop a tank
waving an Uzi, a heroic fighter who could lick a battalion of the
enemy single-handed. I put part of my feelings about this special
nation-state into a Landlord column. It began with Gabriel informing the Landlord that his beloved Irish were being bombed, shot,
burned and clubbed:

> THE LANDLORD: (*sternly*) Who risks my wrath by attacking my
> jolly, lovable Irish?
> GABRIEL: As usual, sir, the Irish.
> THE LANDLORD: (*thoughtfully*) I think it's high time I personally
> intervened down there. I shall wisely adjudicate the dispute
> and thereby demonstrate how all men can live in peace and
> brotherhood.
> GABRIEL: (*nervously*) Frankly, sir, I'd advise against that. The
> issues are rather difficult to . . .
> THE LANDLORD: (*annoyed*) Are you doubting my omnipotence,
> Gabriel? Just tick off the facts, and I'll hand down my verdict.
> Now, just why are the Irish killing each other?
> GABRIEL: Well, basically, sir to determine which are the better
> Christians.
> THE LANDLORD: I beg your pardon, Gabriel?
> GABRIEL: You see, sir, the Protestant majority has been persecut-
> ing the minority Catholics in Northern Ireland for years because
> the Catholics burn candles, drink wine and eat wafers in church.
> THE LANDLORD: Well, that's settled then. Obviously, those who
> would persecute their fellow men for such piddling reasons have
> no concept of what Christianity is all about. I will declare the

Catholics to be the true Christians and have done with it.

GABRIEL: Yes, sir. Does that apply to the Catholic majorities in Spain, South America and elsewhere who have been persecuting Protestant minorities for years because they don't burn candles, drink wine and eat wafers in church?

THE LANDLORD: Good Me, no. Is that all these so-called Christians can do, persecute each other?.

GABRIEL: Oh, no, sir. They also persecute Jews, Moslems, Hindus, Buddhists ...

THE LANDLORD: (*sadly*) Are there no true Christians down there, Gabriel?

GABRIEL: Well, the Jews have been so busy being persecuted over the centuries that they haven't had much time to persecute anyone else.

THE LANDLORD: Good. Then I'll simply declare the Jews to be the true Christians and that's that.

GABRIEL: Yes, sir, but you'd better hurry. Now that they have a Jewish state with an Arab minority...

The suggestion that the Landlord hurry proved prophetic as far as I was concerned. I took a second trip to Israel in 1970. This time I spent two weeks with another bunch of editors and reporters touring the country from Sharm al-Sheikh on the Red Sea to the fortifications looking out at Syria from the Golan Heights. We interviewed Golda Meir, David Ben-Gurion, Shimon Peres and generally behaved like serious news-gatherers. The country had already begun to change. The incredible successes of the Six-Day War had bred a new cockiness. "We were scared to death what with the Lebanese Air Force only five minutes from Tel Aviv," went a typical Israeli joke. "But fortunately, their pilot was sick."

The sense of communality—the *kibbutzim* spirit—was beginning to be diluted. With the economy growing, entrepreneurs were proliferating. And that most noble of crusades, the aliyah, which brought Jews from all over the world to become automatic citizens, was fast producing a distinct and separate lower class, the Sephardim. These were the impoverished and uneducated Jews from the Middle East and North Africa fit only to compete with the Israeli Arabs for the menial jobs. The story was told of one such group who were being flown to Tel Aviv from Yemen in an El Al jet. In mid-flight they purportedly lit a fire in the aisle in the rear to cook the food they had brought along. While the story was perhaps apocryphal, the fact that it was widespread indicated the attitude of the established settlers toward these newcomers.

The interview with Golda Meir, however, was worth a two-week trip to anywhere. She was then at the height of her powers and her Jewish motherliness. When she spoke of the Arabs, the Russians or the United Nations, her heavy shoulders and eyebrows would rise in pained resignation, as though her warm heart found it hard to believe anyone could behave, God forbid, so spitefully. The United States? A kindly uncle, well-intentioned, mind you, but far away—the sort you could count on for a Rosh Hashanah card, some avuncular advice and not much else.

Her Israeli boys, of course, were the finest boys anywhere. To think that anyone should accuse them of taking something that wasn't theirs, like the Sinai Peninsula! "Do people believe we got up one fine morning and said we haven't got enough rocks and desert already?" she asked, her raised palms outward in mock incredulity.

Then, having thus analyzed the situation in the Middle East, she shook each of our hands and asked with a concerned smile: "And are you having a nice time in Israel?"

What a sweet, understanding, compassionate Jewish mother. It was amazing she could be so tender-hearted after surviving three wars and half a century of Middle East politics. It brings to mind the then-current Israeli assessment of her: "Q: When all the politicians are standing on the podium reviewing the troops, how do you tell which one's Golda? A: "She's the one with the balls."

Having become an expert myself on Middle East politics in two weeks, I naturally offered a solution to the morass. The column began by outlining Israel's hopeless situation and spelling out the Letter to the World that Golda Meir wrote. It ended: "So we give up."

The unconditional surrender of Israel stunned the world.
The Arabs were jubilant, the Russians delighted. "In a way,

it's a shame," said the State Department. "But all things considered …"

Almost overlooked in the excitement was the postscript Mrs. Meir had appended to her letter: "P.S. To whom should we surrender?"

"As leader of the Arab world," said President Nasser in a triumphant broadcast from Cairo, "I shall personally go to Jerusalem to accept the abject surrender of the Israelis, whom I have at last brought to their knees."

"You and whose army?" cried the King of Jordan. "My Arabs are legion."

"Look here," said the Syrians, "we have hated the Israelis more than you hated the Israelis. We'll treat them more hatefully than anybody."

And down in the Persian Gulf, such Arab leaders as the Imquat of Qumquat and the Sukhat of Tash angrily demanded a piece of the vengeful action.

But most outraged, of course, were the Palestinian guerrillas, who had been outraged for years. "It's my country," shouted Al Fatah, leader of the dread Palestine Freedom Fighters (PFF), "and I'll lead the victorious forces into my reconquered land."

"Over my dead body," cried his brother, George, head of the dread Freedom Fighters of Palestine (FFP).

"I'll buy that," agreed Al, and they started a war to see who would be the first to overthrow the government of Lebanon, which was handy.

Iraq sided with Al and Libya with George. The Saudis, who despised Iraq more than they despised Libya, invaded Kuwait, which it didn't like either. The Imquat of Qumquat ordered his Royal Air Force to warm up its engine and go bomb Algeria. Syria attacked Egypt and the Crucial Trucial States. Only Yemen remained neutral, not wishing anything to interfere with its 30-year civil war.

Naturally, the sides changed from week to week, that being the way it is in the Middle East. And naturally the Arabs fought on year after year with undiminished vigor, valor and venom, that also being the way it is in the Middle East.

Mrs. Meir said Israel would stand by its pledge to surrender to the proper Arab leader—"even if it takes the Arabs a thousand years to determine who that shall be." When experts said she was being overly optimistic, Mrs. Meir shrugged. "They're happy," she said, "we're happy."

I based that column in part on a fable first told me by an Israel hotel clerk on that '70 trip. For those who haven't yet heard it:

Once upon a time, the Scorpion asked the Frog for a ride across the river on the Frog's back.

"What do you take me for?" said the Frog. "We are mortal enemies. When I get to the middle of the river, you'll stab me in the back."

"Don't be foolish," said the Scorpion. "If I stab you in the back, we'll both drown. What would be the point of that?"

"True," said the Frog. "All right, then, climb aboard."

Once they had reached the middle of the river— POW!—the Scorpion let the Frog have it, smack in the center of his back.

"Now we shall both perish," cried the Frog in its last breaths. "Oh, why did you commit such a foul and irrational act?"

The Scorpion managed one final shrug. "This," it said, as its head disappeared beneath the waters, "is the Middle East."

Since then, the spirit that made Israel unique among nations has faded with each passing year, with each increment in its power. The invasion of Lebanon, the building of settlements in the West Bank, the repressive measures against the Intifada ... All have dimmed its once-glowing image. The satirist Kishon, who wrote so touchingly about Israel's early days, reportedly now lives in Switzerland and has little to do with his native land. Topol still owns a house in Israel but spends most of his time in London, where the living is easier. Today, Israel is just another nation state, better than some maybe, but nothing to write home about. So it's back to the old World Federalism drawing board and yet ... it's lovely to think that there once existed a magical country where the citizens all lived as brothers and sisters in joyous discord—a Jewish Camelot.

Chapter Fourteen

THE NATURE OF MAN, THE ESSENCE OF GOD

AND THE MEANING OF LIFE

All we columnists have our narrow fields of specialization. As for me, I've always stuck pretty much with the nature of man, the essence of God and the meaning of life. Those not interested in such constrained topics would be well advised to skip to Chapter Fifteen, which deals with incest among the great apes.

Actually, I've spent my life writing about chimeras: government, politics, money... I remember when the Republic of South Vietnam collapsed in 1975. Here was a nation of 20 million people. It had an army of a million men. It had an air force, tanks, artillery and tons of ammunition. It had a president and a vast bureaucracy of tax collectors, prosecutors and policemen. It had its own diplomats, its own currency, its own flag. It had everything a sovereign nation requires to be a sovereign nation. For twenty-one years, we believed there was such an entity as the Republic of South Vietnam. To sustain it, we spent more than a billion dollars and 58,000 American lives. Then virtually overnight, it ceased to exist.

A retreat was ordered. The retreat turned into a rout, the rout into a disaster. Soldiers no longer feared their officers and threw down their arms. With no army to protect them, the politicians fled. With no political leaders, the Republic of South Vietnam vanished from the face of the earth. Just like that.

So sovereign nations exist on faith alone. They are created in the minds of the people. They exist only in the minds of the people. They have power over their citizens solely because their citizens believe they have power. This is what we are asked to strive and die for.

Money, too. After all, money is valuable only because we think it's valuable. We used to have faith in these worthless pieces of paper because we dug a heavy yellow metal out of the ground, loaded it on trucks, carried it long distances and then reburied it under the ground. But we don't even bother with that mumbo-jumbo anymore.

Thus many of our cherished institutions are Oz-like fabrications. The stock market is a fine example. I've always thought of the stock market as a mystical beast that controls our lives, yet it's equipped with telepathic powers and blind obedience. It not only knows what we're thinking, but it invariably does whatever we think it should do. If we think it is going up, we buy stocks and it goes up, making us all prosperous and happy. If we think it's going down, we sell stocks and it goes down, leaving us all impoverished and forlorn. If we could all get together every day and simply think it was going up, it would soar interminably, making everyone prosperous and happy forever. Needless to say, that's a ridiculous idea.

So, for much of our lives, we deal with things that don't exist except in our minds. That leads me to death. I used to want to die slowly. When a friend shuffles off this mortal coil in his sleep or keels over on the tennis court, the customary comment is that at least he chose an enviable way to go. "He never knew what hit him," people will say, shaking their heads in awe at this evidence of the Good Lord's boundless mercy.

Nonsense. When I go, I said, I want to go slowly—slowly and, needless to say, painlessly. It's not so much that this would give me time to put my affairs in order (it wouldn't), it's that I want to experience the experience of dying.

Life, after all, is the sum of your experiences. The more you experience, the more you live. When I was young, I argued that Richard Halliburton, who drowned at the age of 39 while attempting to cross the Pacific in a Chinese junk, lived more than my sweet Aunt Jean, who quietly passed away at 84 after a blameless life. Mr. Halliburton swam the Hellespont, scaled the Alps and engaged in all sorts of derring-do. Aunt Jean was active in Christian Science circles. Lucky Mr. Halliburton, I would say, poor Aunt Jean. I'm afraid I've modeled my life more on Aunt Jean's than Mr. Halliburton's. But I treasure what we all treasure—the memory of our experiences.

I wish I could remember being born. That must have been the grandest experience of them all. But I do remember my first kiss, my wedding and holding my first grandchild in my arms. She was (forgive a grandfather) a beautiful child—blue eyes, a shock of black hair and, by some ever-reoccurring miracle, perfectly formed. I held her in my arms, and when I touched the sole of one small foot, her tiny toes curled. I had forgotten about this phenomenon in the new-born. The anthropologists tell us it is a throwback to the prehensile feet of our tree-dwelling ancestors millions of years ago. So there we were, after all these eons, just the two of us—I, the grandfather, approaching the end of my era (with no great haste, mind you) and she at the very dawn of her own. For the first time, I was acutely aware that I was not only part of the millions of years that had been, but also of the millions of years to come. What a richly rewarding feeling.

But dying, of course, is the neat ribbon that ties up my own little package. To die suddenly without warning, without knowledge, is to be cheated of that final experience. It is aesthetically unsound— as though in the middle of the third act of a marvelously contrived play the lights suddenly fail, plunging the theater into darkness. How far better to have a grand exit line and a final curtain as the audience rises in a standing ovation.

With a painless six months, I liked to think I could die well. A few of my friends have died badly, going not gently into the night, but berating their loved ones and cursing fate. Others have accepted their sentences with stoic courage, and I have admired them highly. I'm not sure why it matters so much. I've never given a fig about my funeral arrangements. Once dead, I was sure I wouldn't be much concerned if my mortal remains were scattered ashes, food for the worms or hung up for the crows. I did write a column on the subject. It was based on what I thought was a fine solution:

"And when I go," I said to my dear wife, Glynda, patting her hand fondly, "I want you to promise me you'll remarry."

"Of course," she said.

Of course? That was several weeks ago, and I've been mulling over the matter ever since. In fact I brought it up, somewhat indirectly, the other evening.

"And when I go," I said, "I want to be stuffed."

"I beg your pardon?" said Glynda.

"Cremation is so final," I said. "I just can't think of myself as a little handful of ashes. Burial, on the other hand, is so depressing. Who knows what you're going to run into down there, deep underground. You know how I feel about subways."

"Why don't you leave your body to science?" suggested Glynda. "I'm sure they'd be fascinated with your liver."

"And have a bunch of young medical students making wisecracks over my remains? I don't even care much for men's locker rooms. No, stuffing is the only viable alternative."

Glynda looked pensive. "I suppose I could stand you up in the hall," she said.

"Good heavens, I don't want to stand up through eternity," I said. "I picture myself seated here in my easy chair, wearing a warm, pleasant smile and that comfortable old gray sweater with the leather elbow patches. I think I'd like Gibbons' *Decline and Fall of the Roman Empire* on my lap. I've always been meaning to read it. And perhaps a pipe in my mouth."

"You quit smoking ten years ago," said Glynda.

"It couldn't hurt," I said. "And it's not as though I'll be any trouble to you. All I ask is an occasional whisk with the duster and perhaps a sprig of holly in my buttonhole at Christmas time. Do you think the children will mind my not chatting with them?"

"I don't think they'll notice," said Glynda. "But it could start a fight over their inheritance: 'You get Dad!' 'No, you get Dad!'"

"Very funny," I said. "But I certainly hope you don't feel the sight of me would spoil any of those gala parties you plan to throw when I've gone to the Great Taxidermist in the Sky."

"No," said Glynda, "I'll just say you had your two

martinis early. But I'm constantly amazed at what you writers won't do for immortality. It's too bad your last book didn't sell better."

I decided to ignore that. "What concerns me most, of course," I said, "is how your new husband will take to me. But after all, you wouldn't want him sitting in my chair. And I won't be in the way. You can bill and coo or have your spats, and I won't say a word. I'll just sit there, smiling pleasantly, beloved by one and by all."

"Very thoughtful of you, dear," she said. "I know just the sort of event to have when you arrive home from the taxidermist."

I couldn't help being pleased. "Are you thinking of a simple, but moving, memorial service?" I said.

"No," said Glynda, nibbling on an olive, "a garage sale."

But if I didn't much care about the disposal of my remains, why was I so concerned about dying well? I suppose I saw it as a final legacy, one your family and your friends would remember most vividly. If you did it well, it might well overshadow your failings, perhaps even wiping your slate clean, like the last rites of the Catholics or the execution of Sidney Carton. Ah, how I envied Socrates lying on a hillside, imparting eternal wisdom to his disciples as the hemlock-induced paralysis crept up his legs toward his heart. What a wonderful way to go!

To be sure, I was in no hurry to get there. What constantly surprises me is the vast number of people who are. When someone says to me, "Thank God it's Friday," my shoulders hunch. When we are young, we dwell in a thickened sea of time with no horizon. A sleepless nap hour is interminable. The Fourth of July lasts a month and Christmas Day a year. As children, we can't wait for recess, for the final bell, for Easter vacation. We can't wait to get out of lower school, middle school, high school and college. We can't wait to get out in the world, to get married, to have children and for the children to leave home. We can't wait to get a job, and, when we get one, we count the days until Friday, we count the weeks until vacation, we count the years until retirement. We can't wait.

Thank God it's Friday? But Friday marks the end of another week. All too few weeks are left. How cruel it is that when you are young and burdened with seemingly endless time, it passes with agonizing slowness, and when you are old, no matter how desperately you clutch at it, it hurtles by with mindless callousness.

Thank God it's Friday? Thank God it's any day you wake up to, and I often do. I can't say that I've made my peace with my God; I was never mad at Him. We get along fine. I'm constantly thanking Him for my blessings, which I know are unfairly more than most, and I never beg Him for a favor, except for a loved one in desperate circumstances, but not ever for myself. I find it presumptuous to ask Him to rig the outcome of a football game or to obstruct justice by preventing an officer from tagging my car. It makes me feel good to thank Him and ask nothing in return. It makes me feel like a humble, grateful penitent who walks softly on His earth. Of course, if He should see fit to reward such an admirable attitude with His blessings . . .

So I wanted to die slowly and dramatically, but that was before I realized that I wasn't going to die at all.

I'm not alone in my thinking. I recently asked a friend Chuck Adams if he had thought about estate planning, as it's euphemistically termed. "Well, it really doesn't make much sense," he said, "if you're not going to die." He's wrong, of course. He's going to die. It's I who is not going to die. That's because I am the only one who exists.

Cogito ergo sum. But it's more than "I think, therefore I am." It's "I perceive, therefore you're not." You, the Swedish ivy on my desk and the farthest galaxy exist only in my perceptions. I don't see you; my eyes see only light waves reflected off your surface. I don't hear you shouting, "But I am! I am!" My ear drums are merely reverberating from waves of sound that I interpret as I will. You poke me in the ribs to prove you exist. No, you don't. What exists are my nerve endings registering momentary discomfort. You, the ivy and the cosmos are merely stimuli to my five senses. The stimuli are passed through my neurons to my God-like brain which then creates you and all my works. It is there, and only there, that you exist. Sorry about that.

You may well argue that the same applies to you. Please do. It will make you feel better. Anyway, it's no concern of mine. For me, only I exist, and because only I exist, my death is literally inconceivable. If I were to die, this cosmos that exists only in my mind would die with me. Space and time, both figments of my brain, would cease to exist. We may be able to envision the world going on without us, but we can't envision no us and no world. Just as our finite minds can't deal with the concept of infinity, neither can they deal with the concept of no time and no space. My death, therefore, is literally inconceivable.

It's a pretty conceit, but of small comfort. It's one of those philosophical theses that I believe, but don't believe in. Here's another: There's no free will.

It was an argument I first heard in college. I despised it, first because I believe strongly in the individual and his or her power to stand up to the fates, and second because I could find no way to refute it. This rankled me over the years, on the rare occasions that I thought of it. Finally, I wrote a column setting forth the argument and pleading with readers to help me tear it apart. I received 140 letters from kindly souls all too eager to set me straight. It wasn't so much the volume, which was considerable for a single column; it was that all too many of the letters were two and three pages, single-spaced. Poor Janice Greene.

If you'll forgive a digression, Ms. Greene has been my good right hand since 1980. She is a gentle, hard-working, intelligent woman with a free-running imagination and a fine sense of humor. She's far more than a secretary. Her official title is editorial assistant. She proofreads, thinks up column ideas and answers the mail. When I first became a columnist, I handled the mail like any efficient, high-powered executive: My editorial assistant would open the letters and place them on my desk, I would read them and stick them in her basket. When a number had accumulated, we would have a dictation session. I would read the letter again, dictate an answer, and she would carry it off. After typing up the answer, she would append it to the letter, which I would read for a third time before signing the reply—just like any efficient, high-powered executive. Seeing that most of my incoming mail begins with either a phrase like "That wasn't a bad column you wrote on …" or "You blithering idiot …," I felt there must be a better way. There was: Nowadays, Ms. Greene, who is an excellent writer, opens the mail, reads the letter, types up an answer and places it on my desk. I read the letter once and, nine times out of ten, sign the answer without alterations. My only worry is that if I ever become famous, some scholar will publish *The Collected Letters of Janice Greene.*

In the case of the free-will column, however, Ms. Greene looked at that stack of single-spaced letters and threw up her hands. Nor could I blame her. I waded through them one by one and shuffled despondently out through the same door by which in I went. But let me give you the argument:

First, as the distinguished psychologist B. F. Skinner noted long ago, we are all products of our heredity and environment. Nothing else. And we have no control whatsoever over either. With heredity, this is obvious. Whether we are strong or weak, smart or dumb, handsome or ugly is none of our doing. Our faults, dear Brutus, lie in our genes. The fact that we are vain about our strength, our intelligence or our beauty speaks well for our amazing ability to take credit for the accomplishments of others.

Nor have we any control whatsoever over our environment. We have no say as to what womb harbors us or in what bed we are hatched. The squalling infant squalls because he is a born complainer or because his bottom is pricked with an environmental pin. He doesn't choose to cry. There is no decision-making process at work inside his pristine brain. Whether he cries is determined solely by his environment and his heredity.

His first decisions, then, are purely the results of these two factors and not decisions at all, but simply preordained responses. So is each subsequent one. As he grows, his environment changes, but he has no control whatsoever over each change. Cause and effect. Every effect has a cause, and no effect chooses its cause. Through no effort of his own, our infant is kept warm, he is fed, he is loved. He is confident and secure. Or, through no effort of his own, he is cold, he is hungry, he is abused. He is angry and afraid.

Eventually, he makes his first conscious moral decision. Shall he take a cookie from his younger sister? Does he come from a long line of swaggering bullies? Is he cold, hungry and afraid? He'll take it. Or is he the warm, well-fed, beloved descendant of a pantheon of saints? The issue was never in doubt.

Environment and heredity. Nothing else. Our society, of course, doesn't accept this. In the conventional wisdom, there is some sort of decision-making device in our brains that is independent of environment and heredity. I see it as about the size of a walnut. When a conflict arises, this walnut calmly assesses the factors involved and then logically chooses A over B. But where did this walnut come from? Surely it was inherited along with your ears, toes and other body parts. Were you blessed with a large walnut, capable of making quick, comprehensive and beneficial decisions? Or were you cursed by your progenitors with a shriveled walnut that vacillates interminably before coming up with a disastrous choice? Just as surely, that walnut was influenced by the results of its previous decisions and the experiences that life imposes.

Environment and heredity. Nothing else. No free will. And if there is no free will, there is, of course, no guilt. Actually, society concedes that environment and heredity can diminish free will. In our criminal statutes, the congenital schizophrenic is hospitalized rather than hanged. The battered wife who chops off her husband's penis makes a fortune on the talk shows. Often such defenses fail. Back in 1984, I became emotionally entangled in the case of Alex Cabarga. He was a soft-featured, sloe-eyed youth of 19 at the time. He and his 34-year-old mentor, Luis (Tree Frog) Johnson, were convicted of kidnapping and molesting two young children. It was a despicable crime, and public sympathy was naturally lavished on the innocent victims. At the trial, it developed that Cabarga's parents had abandoned him to Tree Frog Johnson when the boy was nine years old. For the ensuing ten years, Johnson had beaten and sodomized Cabarga almost daily. At his trial, psychiatrists testified that Cabarga had understandably developed "a pathological dependence" on Johnson and, at his behest, had done unto others as had been done unto him. The judge, after listening to all this, threw the book at Cabarga, sentencing him to 208 years in prison, where, despite appeals to justice, he still remains. So sometimes we accept the doctrine of diminished free will and sometimes we don't. Our approach to the subject is appallingly illogical.

All too many of the letters trying to be helpful said the writer recalled making a choice between this or that, and therefore, he or she was blessed with free will. Several said that free will was a gift from an omnipotent God, and, while you can't argue with religious faith, you don't have to accept it either. A very few readers offered extremely convoluted rebuttals that I simply didn't understand. But none convinced me of the error of my logical ways. We can't, of course, conduct our lives as though there were no free will. It might be lovely to sit under a palm tree for the rest of my days, singing "Que Sera Sera," but I must strive with everyone else. I have no choice.

Yet with the new diminished-capacity defenses, we are nibbling our way toward the thesis that every act is the result of a series of causes beyond our control. We are coming a mite closer to accepting the theory that there is no free will. When we do, of course, there will be no guilt whatsoever. No death, no guilt. There, that should make us all feel better.

More good news. We're all members of one big family—you, me and that Swedish ivy. Theories abound on how life began, but I cling happily to the one in which a bolt of lightning strikes a soup of chemicals sloshing about in the hollow of a primordial rock. SHAZAM! A microscopic dot of life is created. Call it Elmer. It grows, it splits, it splits again and again and again. It mutates, again and again and again. For four billion years, Elmer's direct descendants divide, multiply and mutate. So here we are, cousins all—you, me and the Swedish ivy, which has sent a loving tendril to curl around the stapler. It's a delightful thought. The only persons sure to reject it are the upper-class English, who firmly believe they have more ancestors than anyone else.

Eternal life without guilt in a world of oneness. It's a satisfying set of beliefs. I just wish I believed *in* them. Instead, like most of us, I've gone through life guilt-ridden, self-centered and burdened with intimations of my mortality. I was polite enough, however, on reaching 60 to write a thank-you note. It went like this:

> Thank you, God, I've had a marvelous time. It's not that I plan on leaving in the near future. That's up to you. But I've hit three-score lovely years, and I thought it time to write a thank-you note to my host or hostess as the case may be.

It's been a wonderful party, God, absolutely wonderful. It was the guests who made it. I can't say I liked all of them. A few were stuffed shirts, a few were wet blankets and a few badly misbehaved. But they were the exceptions. All in all, it was a grand bunch.

Frankly, I enjoyed my own family the most. Some men are blessed with good wives, some with good children and some with good friends. You trebly blessed me, God.

I realize quite a few of your guests didn't get enough to eat. I'm sorry about that. Your providence was more than sufficient. Somehow, it just didn't seem to get to those in the back. I never could understand why. Some of us ate too much, while some of us were going hungry. I should have done more to pass your abundance around. But no regrets, no regrets.

I liked the music. What's a party without music? I wish I had a better ear for it. I must say, though, that your reasons for offering heavy-metal rock escape me. But the classics and the old show tunes we danced to on summer nights with the soft wind blowing the white curtains into the ballroom—a hundred ballrooms ... "Kiss me once, and kiss me twice and kiss me once again ... Da-dada dah-dah-dah."

And the setting! Oh, there are spots here and there I could do without. I find deserts dull, and there's much too much of Texas. But rational people like deserts and Texans like Texas. You can't please everybody.

I do love your pine forests. I always felt closer to you up there in the pine forests. I would sit on the porch of our cabin and look up the towering trees, up, up, up to that patch of aching, endless blue and say, "Hello, God."

But why did you supply the beetles that kill the pines? Those sere, brown, oh-so-dead trees that leap to your eyes from the dark-green forests. I found it hard to see the point of that, but then I suppose the beetles enjoy the pines too, don't they?

Of course, most of the setting is ocean. I walk upon the hard-packed sand left by the falling tide, mesmerized by the eternal cadence of your waves. I love your vast and mighty oceans in all their infinite variety—except when I'm on small vessels in your storms. Even then, there is a kind of love in the fear of your wrath.

Your wrath. I never quite believed in your wrath. I see you as a kindly and benevolent host concerned with my well-being. I like to think that your pine beetles and your storms and your malevolent microbes have been placed in my path to remind me that it isn't all fun and games. Nor should it be. Sixty years of pure hedonism would shrivel the soul. So thank you, dear God, for the deserts, for Texas and for the pine beetles.

All in all, I've had an absolutely marvelous time.

So I've spent my adult life propounding unbelievable philosophies, interviewing fictitious characters and analyzing the ephemeral illusions for which people strive and die. And, yes, I've had an absolutely marvelous time.